Sacred Synergy at MahaKumbh:

Uniting Spirituality, Science and Technology

Anilesh Mukherjee

SACRED SYNERGY AT MAHAKUMBH
Uniting Spirituality, Science And Technology
Anilesh Mukherjee

© Anilesh Mukherjee

Published in 2025

© Published by

Qurate Books Pvt. Ltd.
Goa 403523, India
www.quratebooks.com
Tel: 1800-210-6527, Email: info@quratebooks.com

ISBN: 978-93-58989-94-6

A harmonious blend of spirituality, scientific exploration, and technological innovation, the MahaKumbh 2025 in Prayagraj stands as a testament to mankind's evolution. This extraordinary event transcends mere tradition, embodying the profound intersection of spiritual enrichment, planetary movements, and digital transformation.

As millions gather to witness this celestial phenomenon, it serves as a dynamic use case for advanced program and project management, showcasing how cutting-edge technology and strategic management principles can be seamlessly integrated into a timeless spiritual practice.

The MahaKumbh 2025 is not only a celebration of human faith but also a beacon of technological growth and digital innovation, exemplifying the transformative power of modern methodologies in orchestrating such a colossal event.

Gratitude & Reflections

This book culminates my experiences, research, observations, knowledge, and personal perspectives, shaped over years of exploration, learning, and introspection. It would not have been possible without the unwavering support and guidance of the incredible people who have influenced my journey.

First and foremost, I express my deepest gratitude to my parents and my wife for unconditional love, patience, and encouragement. Their support has given me the freedom to explore Adhyatm (spirituality), a journey that has profoundly shaped my thoughts and perspectives. Their belief in me has been my anchor, allowing me to question, learn, and grow.

I am immensely thankful to my teachers and professors, whose wisdom and mentorship helped me develop a structured way of thinking and analyzing the world. Their teachings have been instrumental in shaping my approach to problem-solving, strategic thinking, and continuous learning.

My mentor's invaluable insights, encouragement, and guidance played a crucial role in shaping this book. Their thought-provoking discussions, constructive feedback, and unwavering belief in my work gave me the confidence to bring this vision to life.

Lastly, I extend my gratitude to every individual, counsellor, colleague, and friend who has contributed, directly or indirectly, to this journey. Their perspectives and experiences have enriched my understanding, helping me craft a book that I hope will add value to others.

This book is more than just words on paper; it is a reflection of my journey, my learnings, and my vision—one that I am honored to share with you.

Regards
Anilesh Mukherjee

जय श्री राम   ॐ नमः शिवाय   जय श्री राम

"जब मैं था तब हरि नहीं, अब हरि हैं मैं नाहि"

यह दोहा संत कबीर दास जी का है. इसका अर्थ है कि -

जब तक हमारे पास अहंकार था, तब तक हमें ईश्वर का एहसास नहीं हुआ,

लेकिन ईश्वर की प्राप्ति के साथ हमारा अहंकार खत्म हो गया |

"When I was there, there was no Hari, now I am not Hari"

This couplet is of Saint Kabir Das ji. It means that as long as we had ego, we did not realize God, but with the realization of God our ego ended!

MahaKumbh 2025:

A Historic Confluence of Spirituality, Science and Transformation

(Purification of Heart, Mind, Soul, and Body)

The purpose of this book is to document the extraordinary experience of MahaKumbh, a historic event held in Prayagraj, Uttar Pradesh, Bharat (India). This MahaKumbh, occurring after a remarkable span of 144 years—distinct from the Purna Kumbh, which takes place every 12 years—has been an unparalleled spiritual and cultural phenomenon.

Recognized as the largest human gathering in history, MahaKumbh has imparted profound lessons to all who have witnessed or learned about it. As an observer closely following Prayagraj's transformation since the 1980s, I (Anilesh Mukherjee) have had the privilege of experiencing its evolution firsthand. Prayagraj, akin to Varanasi (Kashi/Banaras), is believed to be one of the oldest cities on Earth, divinely designed and deeply rooted in history and spirituality.

Spiritually, Prayagraj holds the esteemed title of *Tirthraj* (King of Pilgrimages), uniquely positioned at the sacred confluence of three major rivers—Ganga, Yamuna, and Saraswati. While the Saraswati River remains unseen, its essence is believed to manifest in the form of wisdom, learning, and the blessings of revered saints and

sages. This sacred meeting point, known as *Sangam*, has been a focal point of devotion for millennia.

Though MahaKumbh is primarily considered a Sanatan Hindu event, a deeper understanding of the Vedas, Upanishads, and Bhagavad Gita reveals its scientific and philosophical significance for all of humanity. It embodies the universal philosophy of *Vasudhaiva Kutumbakam*—the idea that the world is one family—uniting people beyond religious and cultural boundaries.

Numerous world records were set throughout this grand event, and invaluable insights were gained by those who participated or even learned about it through research or word of mouth. It is believed that attending MahaKumbh is a result of one's good deeds from past lives (*Pichla Janam*), making it a rare and divine opportunity.

Witnessing MahaKumbh has been a blessing for me—an opportunity to seek the grace of Maa Ganga and Yamuna and to receive the wisdom of sages and saints. More than just a spiritual experience, this event provided fascinating insights into science, technology, and modern governance. From a project management perspective, MahaKumbh serves as a live case study for mastering Program Management, Lean Six Sigma, and large-scale operations management.

Through this book, I aim to share my research, experiences, observations, and interpretations for the benefit of all. MahaKumbh is not only a convergence of planetary movements, astrology, and Vedantic philosophy but also a testament to the power of digital transformation, artificial intelligence, and exceptional program management.

This MahaKumbh was also referred to as *the Digital MahaKumbh, marking the first time in history that such an event leveraged extensive digital solutions. It stands as a milestone in the 21st century, showcasing humanity's remarkable advancements* in science and technology.

By the conclusion of this book, you will discover numerous real-world applications and case studies that highlight how MahaKumbh 2025 became a groundbreaking event in multiple domains.

A special note of gratitude goes to the Honorable Chief Minister of Uttar Pradesh, Shri Yogi Adityanath, along with his dedicated team, bureaucrats, law enforcement agencies, the municipal corporation, and the entire administration for ensuring the event's success, safety, and smooth execution. Their efforts made MahaKumbh 2025 not only a spiritual milestone but also a masterclass in governance, technology, and management.

9

Table of Contents

5. The Astrological and Celestial Timings of Kumbh Mela

6. Maha Kumbh Mela vs. Purna Kumbh Mela

7. Prayagraj: The Eternal City of Divinity and Knowledge

8. Amrit Snan (Shahi Snan) – The Sacred Amrit Snan of Maha Kumbh Mela 2025

9. The Akharas and Their Role in Kumbh Mela

जय श्री राम   ॐ नमः शिवाय   जय श्री राम

Maha Kumbh 2025:

A Rare Celestial Convergence

&

Its Spiritual Significance

The Maha Kumbh Mela, one of the most sacred and grand spiritual gatherings, occurs once every 144 years, making it a truly rare and historic event. The 2025 Maha Kumbh, held in Prayagraj, Uttar Pradesh, Bharat (India), is particularly significant due to an extraordinary planetary alignment, deeply rooted in Vedic astrology and ancient scriptures. This celestial occurrence amplifies the spiritual potency of the event, drawing millions of seekers from around the world in pursuit of divine blessings and inner transformation.

Key Astrological Alignments of Maha Kumbh 2025:

1. **Jupiter's Transit in Aquarius (*Guru in Kumbha Rashi*):** Jupiter, revered as Guru in Vedic astrology, represents wisdom, spirituality, and divine guidance. During the Maha Kumbh 2025, its transit through Aquarius (Kumbha Rashi) is considered exceptionally auspicious, as it is believed to enhance spiritual awakening, knowledge, and inner harmony. This positioning fosters an ideal environment for seekers to receive celestial wisdom and purification

2. **Sun's Transit in Capricorn (*Surya in Makar Rashi*):** The Sun, symbolizing vitality, authority, and enlightenment, enters Capricorn (Makar Rashi) during this sacred period. This transition is considered a moment of spiritual renewal, marking the beginning of an auspicious cycle of self-discipline, devotion, and transformation. It aligns with the traditional observance of Makar Sankranti, reinforcing the belief that bathing in the holy waters during this time purifies the soul and bestows divine grace

3. **Moon's Transit Through Sacred Nakshatras:** The Moon, governing emotions, mind, and consciousness, moves through various Nakshatras (lunar constellations) during the Maha

Kumbh, further amplifying the event's spiritual energy. These lunar transitions are believed to intensify the effects of meditation, prayers, and rituals performed at the sacred confluence (*Sangam*) of the Ganga, Yamuna, and the spiritual Saraswati rivers

4. **The Rare Alignment of the Sun, Moon, Jupiter, and Saturn:** What makes the 2025 Maha Kumbh exceptionally rare is its unique alignment of four major celestial bodies—the Sun, Moon, Jupiter, and Saturn. This planetary combination, occurring once in 144 years, was deeply connected to the cosmic phenomenon of Samudra Manthan (the churning of the ocean) described in the Vishnu Purana. According to ancient wisdom, this alignment creates an energetic gateway for unparalleled spiritual elevation, karmic cleansing, and divine blessings

The Spiritual and Mystical Significance

These rare planetary movements are believed to create a divinely charged atmosphere, making Maha Kumbh 2025 an extraordinary opportunity for spiritual purification, enlightenment, and transcendence. Devotees, saints, and seekers from across the globe gather at Prayagraj to take the holy dip at Sangam, believing that the sacred waters absorb the celestial energies, thereby cleansing sins and bestowing moksha (liberation).

Maha Kumbh was not merely a religious congregation but a harmonious confluence of astronomy, spirituality, and ancient wisdom, reinforcing the Sanatan Dharma principle of universal well-being and cosmic interconnectedness.

This celestial event, guided by timeless astrological wisdom, makes Maha Kumbh 2025 a once-in-a-lifetime spiritual phenomenon—an invitation for every soul to embark on a journey of self-discovery, divine connection, and eternal transformation.

Samudra Manthan: The Cosmic Churning of the Ocean

A Divine Episode in Sanatan Scriptures

Samudra Manthan, or the Churning of the Ocean, stands as one of the most profound and symbolic episodes in Sanatan Dharma. It is extensively described in the Bhagavata Purana, Vishnu Purana, and the Mahabharata, portraying the eternal struggle between good and evil, the pursuit of divine wisdom, and the cosmic balance of power. The event was conducted to obtain Amrit (the nectar of immortality) but was triggered by a chain of events set into motion by Indra's arrogance.

The Origin: Why Did Samudra Manthan Happen?

The story begins with Indra, the king of Devas, ruling over Swarga (Heaven). One day, Sage Durvasa, known for his unpredictable temper, presented Indra with a divine garland. However, in an act of arrogance, Indra carelessly placed the garland on his elephant, Airavata, which, unaware of its sanctity, trampled it underfoot. Enraged by this disrespect toward divine blessings, Sage Durvasa cursed Indra and all the Devas, causing them to lose their strength, prosperity, and celestial glory. With the Devas weakened, the Asuras, led by King Bali, saw an opportunity to conquer the three worlds. Overwhelmed and powerless, the Devas sought divine intervention.

The Divine Plan: Who Suggested Samudra Manthan?

In their desperation, Indra and the Devas approached Lord Brahma, who then guided them to Lord Vishnu, the preserver of the universe. Vishnu revealed that Amrit, hidden in the depths of Ksheer Sagar (the Ocean of Milk), had the power to restore the Devas' strength and immortality.

However, retrieving the nectar required immense effort. Since the weakened Devas lacked the strength for such a task, Vishnu advised them to ally with the Asuras, promising them a share of the nectar in return for their cooperation. Despite their distrust, the Asuras, tempted by the prospect of immortality, agreed.

The Process: How Was Samudra Manthan Performed?

The churning of the ocean was an extraordinary celestial event, requiring immense power and sacred elements:

1. Mandara Mountain as the Churning Rod – The Devas and Asuras used the massive Mandara Mountain as the churning rod

2. Vasuki, the King of Serpents, as the Churning Rope – The serpent Vasuki, belonging to Lord Shiva, served as the rope to rotate the mountain

3. Kurma Avatar of Vishnu – As the mountain began sinking into the ocean's depths, Lord Vishnu incarnated as Kurma (the Divine Tortoise) to support it on his back

As they churned the ocean, several celestial and mystical objects emerged, each carrying divine significance.

The Gifts of Samudra Manthan: Divine and Cosmic Treasures

As the ocean was churned with immense force, numerous celestial and formidable entities emerged, each carrying profound significance:

1. **Halahala (The Deadly Poison)** – The first substance to surface was a highly potent poison, so destructive that it threatened to annihilate the universe. To prevent catastrophe, Lord Shiva consumed the poison, and Goddess Parvati held it in his throat, causing it to turn blue, earning him the title Neelkanth (The Blue-Throated One)

2. **Kamadhenu (The Divine Cow)** – A celestial cow with the ability to provide an inexhaustible supply of milk. Kamadhenu was imbued with divine blessings and was given to sages to support humanity's welfare. The cow holds deep spiritual and practical significance, symbolizing nourishment, prosperity, and selfless service. In ancient times, it was revered as Dhenu, meaning one who grants wishes, and is still considered sacred in Hindu traditions

3. **Uchchaihshravas (The Seven-Headed Celestial Horse)** – A magnificent, snow-white horse that emerged from the churning and was claimed by Indra, the ruler of Swarga (Heaven)

4. **Airavata (The Divine White Elephant)** – A majestic elephant with immense strength and purity, chosen by Indra as his celestial mount. Airavata symbolizes royalty, power, and auspiciousness

5. **Kaustubha (The Radiant Gem)** – A dazzling and unparalleled jewel that found its place adorning Lord Vishnu. Legends say that such a gem now remains only with the mystical Nāgas (serpents). It is believed that when Lord Krishna subdued Kaliya Nag, the serpent surrendered this gem to him in reverence

6. **Kalpavriksha (The Wish-Fulfilling Tree)** – A celestial tree with the power to grant any wish. It was placed in Indra's divine paradise, signifying abundance and eternal blessings

7. **Apsaras (Celestial Dancers)** – Enchanting divine nymphs, including Rambha, emerged, epitomizing beauty, grace, and artistic expression. They became part of Indra's royal court. These celestial beings are associated with divine entertainment and are believed to reside in Gandharvaloka

8. **Goddess Lakshmi (The Embodiment of Prosperity)** – The churning also brought forth Goddess Lakshmi, symbolizing wealth, fortune, and auspiciousness. It is believed that in homes where women are honored and respected, prosperity prevails. She was reunited with Lord Vishnu, and her return is celebrated annually on Diwali (Kartik Amavasya)

9. **Varuni Devi (The Goddess of Water and Wine)** – A divine entity linked to celestial liquor, Varuni was taken by the Asuras. This liquor, derived from Kadamba fruits, is also referred to as Varuni

10. **Mrigank (The Moon)** – The luminous Moon also arose from the depths of the ocean. Since it originated from water, it is often referred to as a water planet. The Moon was bestowed upon Lord Shiva, who placed it upon his head, further solidifying his celestial connection

11. **Parijata (The Divine Flowering Tree)** – Alongside Kalpavriksha, the Parijat tree emerged, renowned for its exquisite and fragrant blossoms. These sacred flowers hold deep spiritual significance in Hindu worship and are revered for their medicinal properties. Goddess Lakshmi is particularly fond of Parijat flowers

12. **Panchjanya (The Divine Conch)** – Considered one of the 14 celestial gems, Panchjanya emerged from the ocean and was dedicated to Lord Vishnu. The conch is a symbol of victory, prosperity, peace, and divine sound. It plays a crucial role in sacred rituals, especially in Lakshmi-Vishnu puja

13. **Dhanvantari (The Divine Physician and Father of Ayurveda)** – Lord Dhanvantari, an incarnation of Lord Vishnu, emerged holding a pot of Amrit (nectar of immortality). He is revered as the father of Ayurveda, having imparted its knowledge to sages and physicians for the well-being of humanity

14. **Amrit (The Nectar of Immortality)** – The ultimate prize of Samudra Manthan, Amrit granted immortality to those who consumed it. As soon as it appeared, the Asuras seized it, leading to a cosmic battle. Lord Vishnu, in his Mohini form, skill-fully ensured that the nectar was consumed only by the Devas

Each manifestation holds deep spiritual and symbolic meaning, illustrating profound lessons on balance, perseverance, and divine intervention in the cosmic order.

The Battle for Amrit: The Deception of Mohini

As soon as the Amrit surfaced, the Asuras seized it, refusing to share it with the Devas. Lord Vishnu took the form of Mohini, a celestial enchantress to reclaim it. Mesmerized by her beauty, the Asuras handed her the nectar, unaware of her intentions. Mohini skillfully distributed the nectar to the Devas while deceiving the Asuras.

However, Rahu, an Asura in disguise, managed to drink the nectar. Before it could take full effect, Lord Vishnu beheaded him with his Sudarshan Chakra, creating the celestial entities Rahu and Ketu— the shadow planets that influence astrological events to this day.

The Legacy of Samudra Manthan

Samudra Manthan represents the eternal struggle between righteousness (Devas) and ego-driven ambition (Asuras). It highlights the importance of perseverance, unity, and divine intervention in restoring cosmic balance.

The event not only restored the Devas' strength and rule over Swarga but also bestowed upon the world profound wisdom, celestial treasures, and the eternal pursuit of spiritual enlightenment. The legend of Samudra Manthan remains a timeless lesson of selfless efforts, resilience, and the triumph of divine order over chaos.

The Amrit Kalash: A Divine Manifestation of Cosmic Churning

The Amrit Kalash refers to the sacred vessel containing Amrit, the divine nectar of immortality, which emerged during the great cosmic churning known as Samudra Manthan. This celestial event symbolized the eternal struggle between righteousness and unrighteousness, as Devas (celestial beings) and Asuras (demons) vied for the nectar's life-bestowing power. In the ensuing battle, a few drops of this elixir fell upon four specific locations on Earth and twelve celestial realms in Swarg Lok (Heaven).

The Distribution of Amrit and Lord Vishnu's Divine Intervention

As the conflict over the Amrit Kalash escalated, Lord Vishnu intervened, assuming his enchanting Mohini form. He strategically distributed the nectar among the Devas with unparalleled grace and wisdom, ensuring their immortality and restoring cosmic equilibrium. However, during this celestial event, a few drops of Amrit inadvertently spilled onto Earth and twelve divine locations in Swarg Lok, sanctifying them for eternity.

The Four Sacred Locations on Earth (Bhoomi Lok)

The four revered sites where the Amrit droplets fell are:

1. **Prayagraj (Uttar Pradesh, Bharat)**

2. **Haridwar (Uttarakhand, Bharat)**

3. **Ujjain (Madhya Pradesh, Bharat)**

4. **Nashik (Maharashtra, Bharat)**

These sacred locations became the focal points for Kumbh Mela, Ardh Kumbh, and Maha Kumbh, and they celebrated cyclically to honor this divine event.

The Twelve Celestial Locations in Swarg Lok

According to Sanatan texts, Amrit also spilled in twelve celestial realms within Swarg Lok. While their exact names remain largely symbolic, these divine abodes are believed to be home to celestial beings, sages, and divine energies that sustain the cosmic order. These sacred locations represent the realms where immortality, divine wisdom, and eternal dharma prevail.

In-Depth Insights into the Four Sacred Earthly Sites

1. Prayagraj (Uttar Pradesh, Bharat)

- **Spiritual Significance:** This revered city hosts the Triveni Sangam, the confluence of the Ganga, Yamuna, and the mystical Saraswati rivers. It is believed that bathing here during Kumbh Mela cleanses all sins and grants Moksha (liberation)

- **Historic & Religious Importance:** Sage Markandeya and various Rishis performed intense penance at this site. It is also the epicenter of Yajnas (sacred rituals) in Sanatan Dharma

- **Kumbh Celebrations:**

    o **Maha Kumbh Mela:** Every 144 years (12 Purna Kumbh cycles)

- o **Purna Kumbh Mela:** Every 12 years

- o **Ardh Kumbh Mela:** Every 6 years

- o **Magh Mela (Mini Kumbh):** Annually during Magh month (January-March)

2. Haridwar (Uttarakhand, Bharat)

- **Spiritual Significance:** This is where the Ganga River enters the plains from the Himalayas. The sacred Har Ki Pauri ghat is believed to be the precise spot where Amrit fell

- **Religious Importance:** Haridwar is closely associated with King Bhagirath, who brought the Ganga from the heavens to Earth. Lord Vishnu's footprint is said to be imprinted on a stone at Har Ki Pauri

- **Kumbh Celebrations:**

  - o **Purna Kumbh Mela:** Every 12 years

  - o **Ardh Kumbh Mela:** Every 6 years

3. Ujjain (Madhya Pradesh, Bharat/India)

- **Spiritual Significance:** Ujjain is the sacred abode of Lord Mahakal (Shiva) and is situated on the banks of the Shipra (Kshipra) River

- **Religious Importance:** It is believed that Lord Vishnu himself dropped Amrit here. Ujjain is also noted for its astronomical significance, as it lies along the Tropic of Cancer

- **Kumbh Celebrations:**

  o **Simhastha Kumbh Mela:** Every 12 years

4. Nashik (Maharashtra, Bharat/India)

- **Spiritual Significance:** Situated along the Godavari River, also known as Dakshin Ganga (Southern Ganges), Nashik holds deep spiritual significance

- **Religious Importance:** It is associated with Lord Rama's exile in the Dandakaranya forest. The region of Panchavati, near Nashik, is where Ravana abducted Sita. The presence of Amrit sanctified the Godavari River

- **Kumbh Celebrations:**

  o **Purna Kumbh Mela:** Every 12 years

The Astrological and Celestial Timings of Kumbh Mela

Kumbh Mela is governed by the planetary positions of Jupiter (Brihaspati) and the Sun in specific zodiac signs:

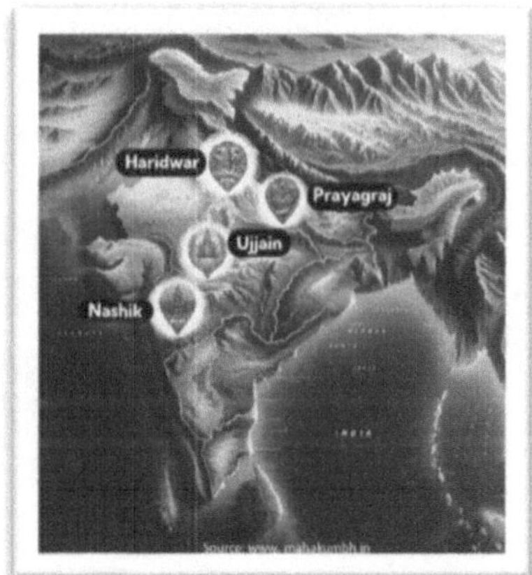

- **Prayagraj:** Jupiter in Taurus, Sun in Capricorn

- **Haridwar:** Jupiter in Aquarius, Sun in Aries

- **Ujjain:** Jupiter in Leo (Simha Rashi)

- **Nashik:** Jupiter and Sun in Leo

Kumbh Mela Cycle

1. **Maha Kumbh Mela** – Every 144 years (Prayagraj only)

2. **Purna Kumbh Mela** – Every 12 years (Rotating among the four locations)

3. **Ardh Kumbh Mela** – Every 6 years (Held at Prayagraj and Haridwar)

4. **Simhastha Kumbh Mela** – Every 12 years (Held in Ujjain)

5. **Magh Mela (Mini Kumbh)** – Annual (Held in Prayagraj during Magh month)

The Profound Significance of Kumbh Mela

The Kumbh Mela serves as a spiritual re-enactment of the cosmic churning, symbolizing the eternal battle between virtue and vice -

- Immersing in the holy rivers during Kumbh is thought to purify the soul, erase past transgressions, impart spiritual enlightenment, and lead one toward liberation (Moksha)
- The grand spiritual gathering attracts millions, including saints, ascetics, and seekers, making it the most significant religious assembly on the planet

Understanding Moksha

Moksha is the ultimate goal of spiritual liberation, transcending the cycle of birth, death, and rebirth.

- **Salokya Mukti:** Residing in the divine realm of one's deity

- **Samipya Mukti:** Being close to the divine

- **Sarupya Mukti:** Attaining the same divine form

- **Sanatan scriptures** declare that Lord Narayana, Mahadeva, and Devi Durga bestow Moksha upon true seekers

The Amrit Kalash and Kumbh Mela represent one of the most profound celestial and spiritual occurrences in Sanatan. The belief that Amrit sanctified these four earthly locations has made them the holiest pilgrimage sites, uniting millions in devotion, faith, and cosmic harmony. The tradition of Kumbh, spanning millennia, is a testament to the timeless wisdom, celestial alignment, and spiritual depth of Sanatan heritage.

Maha Kumbh Mela

vs.

Purna Kumbh Mela

Kumbh Mela: The Pinnacle of Spiritual Congregation

Kumbh Mela is one of the most revered and sacred spiritual gatherings, deeply embedded in Sanatan traditions, astrology, and religious significance. Celebrated at four key locations in Bharat (India)—Prayagraj (Allahabad), Haridwar, Ujjain, and Nashik—this grand festival is a convergence of faith, devotion, and celestial alignments. Among its various forms, the Maha Kumbh and Purna Kumbh stand out as the most significant, each carrying its own spiritual magnitude and astrological precision.

1. Maha Kumbh Mela

An Event of Unparalleled Significance

The Maha Kumbh Mela is the rarest and most spiritually profound gathering, occurring once every 144 years at Prayagraj. This grand event marks the culmination of 12 full Purna Kumbh cycles, making it a once-in-a-lifetime spiritual opportunity for devotees. It witnesses an immense congregation of saints, ascetics, and millions of pilgrims who partake in ritualistic bathing at the sacred Triveni Sangam—the

confluence of the Ganga, Yamuna, and the mystical Saraswati rivers. The holy dip during this period is believed to cleanse all past sins and pave the path toward Moksha (liberation).

Spiritual and Celestial Significance

- **Supreme Purification:** Bathing in the sacred rivers during this celestial period is said to liberate devotees from the cycle of birth and rebirth

- **Cosmic Convergence:** This grand event signifies the highest spiritual energy concentration, occurring after the completion of 12 Purna Kumbh cycles

- **Assembly of Saints and Ascetics:** Renowned Akhadas, sadhus, and sages from across the world gather to impart spiritual wisdom and lead devotional rituals

- **Astrological Rarity:** Occurs when Jupiter aligns in Aries while the Sun is in Capricorn, an alignment that manifests only once in 144 years

Historical Maha Kumbh Celebrations

- **1014 CE:** Early records indicate a grand congregation

- **1156 CE:** Documented by Persian scholar Al-Biruni

- **1954:** The first Maha Kumbh Mela post-independence

- **2001:** The largest recorded gathering, with over 70 million attendees

- **Next Event:** Scheduled to occur in 2145

Key Features of Maha Kumbh Mela

- **Duration:** Spanning approximately 1.5 to 2 months, beginning in January and concluding by March

- **Largest Religious Assembly:** Known as the world's largest spiritual gathering

- **Amrit Snan (Shahi Snan):** Marked by grand processions

of Naga Sadhus and revered saints, performing auspicious ceremonial dips

- **Spiritual Activities:** Includes devotional prayers, religious discourses, yajnas, meditation sessions, and grand Ganga Aartis

2. Purna Kumbh Mela

The Cycle of Spiritual Renewal

Purna Kumbh Mela, commonly referred to as Kumbh Mela, occurs every 12 years at all four sacred sites—Prayagraj, Haridwar, Ujjain, and Nashik. This grand spiritual event is determined by specific planetary alignments, which are believed to bestow divine blessings and purification upon participants.

Spiritual and Astrological Importance

- **Symbolic of Cosmic Struggles:** Represents the eternal battle between Devas and Asuras over the divine nectar, symbolizing the triumph of righteousness

- **Cycle of Purification:** Devotees believe that immersing in the sacred rivers during this time eradicates past karma and accelerates spiritual progress

- **Astrological Significance:** The event is governed by the celestial positioning of Jupiter, the Sun, and the Moon, making each Kumbh Mela unique

Purna Kumbh Locations & Astrological Alignments

Location	Astrological Position
Prayagraj	Jupiter in Taurus, Sun in Capricorn
Haridwar	Jupiter in Aquarius, Sun in Aries
Ujjain	Jupiter in Leo
Nashik	Jupiter and Sun in Leo

Historical Significance of Purna Kumbh

- **7th Century CE:** Earliest records of a grand congregation hosted by Emperor Harsha

- **Continued Tradition:** The event has been observed for centuries, attracting an increasing number of devotees

- **Next Event:** Scheduled for 2037 in Prayagraj

Key Features of Purna Kumbh Mela

- **Duration:** Lasts around 45-60 days

- **Scale:** While massive, it is smaller compared to Maha Kumbh Mela

- **Spiritual Importance:** A highly revered event, facilitating deep spiritual rejuvenation

- **Amrit Snan (Shahi Snan):** Processions of saints and Akhadas mark the most auspicious bathing days

- **Religious and Cultural Activities:** Includes sacred dips, discourses by spiritual leaders, yajnas, and cultural performances

4. Key Differences Between Maha Kumbh and Purna Kumbh

Criteria	Maha Kumbh Mela	Purna Kumbh Mela
Frequency	Once every 144 years	Once every 12 years
Location	Only in Prayagraj	All four locations (Prayagraj, Haridwar, Ujjain, Nashik)
Astrological Condition	Jupiter in Aries, Sun in Capricorn	Varies per location (Jupiter & Sun's position)
Significance	Considered the rarest and holiest gathering	Still significant but more frequent
Duration	1.5-2 months	45-60 days
Number of Attendees	Hundreds of millions	Tens of millions
Spiritual Importance	Represents the culmination of 12 Purna Kumbhs	Individual cycle of renewal

Both the Maha Kumbh and Purna Kumbh hold profound religious and spiritual importance, attracting millions of pilgrims from across the globe. While the Purna Kumbh occurs regularly every 12 years, offering periodic spiritual purification, the Maha Kumbh is an unparalleled event, unfolding once in 144 years, symbolizing the highest form of cosmic and spiritual alignment.

Participating in these sacred events is believed to cleanse the soul, remove karmic burdens, and bring one closer to ultimate liberation. Kumbh Mela, in all its forms, continues to stand as a testament to the enduring faith, devotion, and cultural heritage of Sanatan traditions.

Prayagraj: The Eternal City of Divinity and Knowledge

Prayagraj, formerly known as Allahabad, is one of the world's most ancient and sacred cities. Considered the oldest living city on Earth, it holds immense religious, spiritual, historical, and cultural significance in Sanatan/Hinduism.

The city's ancient name, Prayag, reflects its long-standing status as a major pilgrimage center. According to Hindu scriptures and the Vedic texts, Prayagraj holds a special place in the cosmic order.

It is the Tapo Bhumi (land of penance) of the Rishis and Devas, the Sangam (confluence) of three sacred rivers, and the primary seat of Kumbh and Maha Kumbh Mela.

1. Prayagraj in Ancient Times – Vedic, Spiritual, and Scriptural References

1.1 The Name "Prayagraj"

- The name Prayagraj comes from "Prayag", which means "the foremost Yagna (sacred fire ritual)" / "place of offering" and "Raj", meaning "king"

- It is regarded as the King of Tirthas (holy pilgrimage sites)

- It is also called Tirthraj Prayag, meaning "the supreme pilgrimage" among all other sacred places

1.2 References in Hindu Scriptures

(A) Rigveda (Oldest Hindu Scripture - 1500 BCE or earlier)

- The Rigveda describes Prayag as the holiest site where the confluence of rivers exists, symbolizing spiritual purification. The Vedas, particularly the Rigveda, mention

Prayagraj as a significant site for rituals and offerings to the gods

(B) Manusmriti & Matsya Purana

- Manusmriti calls Prayagraj "the place where gods performed Yagnas" before the creation of the world

- Matsya Purana states that Brahma performed the first Yagna (sacrifice) here, making it the most sacred site in Hindu cosmology

(C) Mahabharata (Vana Parva, Chapter 85-86)

- Lord Krishna described Prayagraj as the holiest place to Yudhishthira and suggested that taking a bath at the Sangam would remove all sins

- It was also at Prayag that Maharishi Bharadwaj established his great Ashram, which became a center of Vedic learning

(D) Ramayana

- Lord Ram, Lakshman, and Sita visited Maharishi Bharadwaj's Ashram at Prayagraj during their exile before proceeding to Chitrakoot

- The Bharadwaj Ashram is still revered in modern Prayagraj

(E) Skanda Purana

- It describes Prayagraj as a place where even Devas (celestial beings) aspire to visit due to its immense spiritual merit

(F) Bhagavata Purana & Vishnu Purana

- These scriptures state that Prayagraj is the only place where all gods reside during the holy month of Magh

- Bathing in the Sangam during Kumbh is equivalent to performing 100 Ashwamedha Yagnas

(G) Triveni Sangam: The most sacred aspect of Prayagraj is the Triveni Sangam, the confluence of three rivers: the Ganga, the Yamuna, and the mystical Saraswati. This confluence is considered the holiest of tirthas (sacred crossing points)

2. Historical Importance – The Oldest City in the World

Prayagraj is often referred to as one of the oldest continuously inhabited cities in the world, alongside Varanasi and Ayodhya. Several historical accounts support this:

2.1 Accounts from Ancient Travelers

- **Hiuen Tsang (7th Century CE, Chinese traveler)** described Prayagraj as a flourishing city, full of scholars, saints, and spiritual seekers

- **Al-Biruni (Persian Historian, 1030 CE)** mentioned that Prayagraj was an important center for Hindu pilgrimages and knowledge

2.2 Mauryan & Gupta Period (4th Century BCE - 5th Century CE)

- Prayagraj has been a center of political and cultural importance since the Maurya and Gupta periods (circa 4th century BCE to 6th century CE). It was known as Kaushambi during the Mauryan era

- Emperor Ashoka (3rd century BCE) built a pillar (Ashoka Pillar) at Prayagraj, which still stands at Allahabad Fort

- Prayagraj was a major center of learning during the Gupta Empire (320-550 CE), considered the Golden Age of India

2.3 Mughal and British Rule

Emperor Akbar (1575 CE) renamed Prayagraj to "Illahabad" (later anglicized to Allahabad), meaning "City of God"

- British rulers recognized it as a key center and established the Allahabad High Court and the University of Allahabad (1887), one of India's oldest universities

2.4 British Colonial Period: During British rule, Allahabad served as an administrative center and played a significant role in the Indian independence movement

3. Present-Day Prayagraj: Geography & Significance

Prayagraj, a major city in Uttar Pradesh, Bharat (India), serves as the administrative headquarters of the Prayagraj district and division. With a population of approximately 1.5 million as per recent estimates, it is one of the largest urban centers in the state. Spread across an area of about 5,482 square kilometres, the district comprises several tehsils, including Sadar, Phulpur, Karchhana, and Bara, making it a key administrative and economic region.

Positioned strategically along the banks of the Ganga and Yamuna rivers, Prayagraj plays a crucial role in trade, commerce, and governance. The city is an educational hub, housing esteemed institutions like Allahabad University, MNNIT, and IIIT. Additionally, its modern infrastructure, including a revamped airport, expressways, and metro connectivity plans, contributes to its development as a key urban center. Despite its rapid urbanization, Prayagraj retains its cultural and historical charm, making it a unique blend of tradition and progress.

3.1 Geographical Location

- Located in Uttar Pradesh, Prayagraj lies at the confluence (Sangam) of three sacred rivers:

    o Ganga (Purity & Liberation)

- o Yamuna (Compassion & Devotion)

- o Saraswati (Wisdom & Knowledge-Invisible River)

- It is situated near Varanasi (~120 km) and Ayodhya (~150 km), forming a holy trinity of sacred Hindu sites

3.2 Spiritual Significance

- Kumbh Mela's Spiritual Center: It is the only city where Maha Kumbh occurs once in 144 years and is the most important location for Purna Kumbh every 12 years

- Tapo Bhumi (Land of Austerity): Saints and sages from ancient times have meditated here, and it remains a spiritual hub today

- Key Temples and Ashrams:

- o Bade Hanuman Ji Temple (Underground temple of Lord Hanuman at Sangam)

- o Alopi Devi Temple (A Shaktipeeth where Sati's hand is believed to have fallen). Located near the confluence of the Ganga, Yamuna, and Saraswati rivers, also known as Prayag Shakti Peeth, dedicated to Goddess Lalith and it's part of the Ashta Das Shaktipeetah concept, which is popular in South India

- o Lalita Devi Temple (A Shaktipeeth where Sati Mata's finger is believed to have fallen). A 108-foot tall, dome-shaped temple that is situated near the river Yamuna, the temple has a large complex that includes a peepal tree, and statues of Rama, Lakshman, Sita, Radha-Krishna, and Hanuman

o Akshayavat (The immortal banyan tree inside Allahabad Fort, believed to grant Moksha). Akshayvat is recognized as a part of Kalpavriksha among the 14 gems obtained from Samudra Manthan. It is believed that Brahma, Vishnu and Mahesh reside in this tree. Akshay Vat is considered to be the visible form of Veni Madhav, the protector of Tirtharaj Prayagraj, Shri Hari Vishnu

o Nagvasuki Temple: The Nagvasuki Mandir in Prayagraj, Uttar Pradesh is a Hindu temple dedicated to the snake god Vasuki. The temple's history is linked to the churning of the ocean of milk in Vedic times. The temple is believed to have originated when Vasuki rested at Prayag after churning the ocean of milk. The temple's idol was established by Lord Brahma's sons. The temple is located on the northwestern bank of the Triveni Sangam. The temple has traditional Hindu architecture with a main hall and sanctum, the sanctum houses a 5-hooded Vasuki idol, and the temple complex also includes deities like Shiva, Goddess Parvati, and Ganesha

4. Why is Maha Kumbh Celebrated Only in Prayagraj?

4.1 Spiritual Reason

- During the Samudra Manthan, when Devas and Asuras fought over Amrit, Lord Vishnu (in Mohini form) carried the Amrit Kalash and four drops fell at four locations:

  o Prayagraj (Allahabad)
  o Haridwar
  o Ujjain
  o Nashik

- Among these, Prayagraj is the most significant, as it is the Triveni Sangam, the holiest confluence of sacred rivers, and is mentioned extensively in Vedic texts.

4.2 Astrological Reason

- Maha Kumbh occurs when Jupiter is in Aries and the Sun is in Capricorn, a unique planetary alignment happening only once every 144 years at Prayagraj

- This alignment enhances the spiritual vibrations and purifying power of the Sangam

4.3 Historical and Cultural Importance

- Emperor Harsha (7th century CE) was the first recorded ruler to organize a grand Kumbh at Prayagraj, setting the tradition

- Over the centuries, Hindu kings, saints, and religious leaders have strengthened its role as the center of Kumbh celebrations

Prayagraj, the oldest, holiest, and most spiritually significant city, continues to be a beacon of Hindu culture, knowledge, and devotion. It is not just a place; it is a living embodiment of Sanatan Dharma's timeless wisdom. Its historical depth, religious sanctity, and cosmic significance make it the most revered pilgrimage site in Hinduism.

Whether during Maha Kumbh, Purna Kumbh, or Magh Mela, Prayagraj remains the gateway to Moksha, where millions gather to seek the blessings of divinity, wisdom, and liberation.

Amrit Snan–

The Sacred Amrit Snan (Shahi Snan) of Maha Kumbh Mela 2025

The Amrit Snan (Shahi Snan), stands as the most revered and spiritually significant ritual of the Maha Kumbh Mela, symbolizing purification, renewal, and divine connection. Held at the Triveni Sangam—the confluence of the Ganga, Yamuna, and the mystical Saraswati in Prayagraj—this ritual bath is believed to absolve one of past sins and accelerate the journey toward Moksha (liberation).

Spiritual Significance of Amrit Snan (Shahi Snan)

The Amrit Snan (Shahi Snan) holds immense spiritual and cosmic importance. According to ancient traditions, the celestial alignment

of the Sun, Moon, and Jupiter during the Kumbh Mela creates an extraordinary spiritual energy field, making the river waters particularly potent for purification. Bathing during this period is thought to not only cleanse an individual's karma but also break the cycle of rebirth, guiding them toward spiritual elevation.

The event is marked by grand processions led by revered Akhadas (sects of saints, sages, and ascetics). These spiritual leaders, often adorned with sacred ash and Rudraksha beads, march toward the holy rivers, symbolizing the triumph of righteousness over negativity. This transformative ritual is not merely an act of bathing—it is a sacred spiritual awakening that reshapes an individual's inner consciousness, aligning them with divine energies.

Amrit Snan (Shahi Snan) Dates for Maha Kumbh Mela 2025

The Maha Kumbh Mela 2025 in Prayagraj witnessed several sacred bathing days, each aligned with key astrological events that amplify their spiritual benefits:

1. Paush Purnima (January 13th, 2025)

The first auspicious bathing day falls on Paush Purnima, a full moon day that marks the beginning of Kalpavas—a month-long period of austerity, meditation, and devotion. The celestial brightness of the full moon is seen as a symbol of purity and inner peace, illuminating the path of self-reflection and spiritual discipline

2. Makar Sankranti (January 14th, 2025) – First Amrit Snan (Shahi Snan)

This day marks the Sun's transition into Capricorn (Makar Rashi) and signifies the beginning of longer and brighter days, symbolizing the victory of light over darkness. The first and most significant Amrit Snan (Shahi Snan) takes place on this day, led by prominent Akhadas and saints, who take the ceremonial plunge at Triveni Sangam. It is believed that this bath removes ignorance, dispels negativity, and rejuvenates the soul

3. Mauni Amavasya (January 29th, 2025) – Most Powerful Bathing Day

Observed on the new moon day, Mauni Amavasya is regarded as the most powerful bathing day of the Kumbh Mela. The word 'Mauni' originates from 'Maun' (silence), and on this day, devotees observe both fasting and silence as a means of self-purification. It is believed that taking a holy dip on Mauni Amavasya not only erases past sins but also enhances one's speech, bringing wisdom, clarity, and eloquence

4. Basant Panchami (February 3rd, 2025) – The Festival of Knowledge

Basant Panchami heralds the arrival of spring and is dedicated to Goddess Saraswati, the deity of knowledge, wisdom, and creativity. Devotees wear yellow attire, offer prayers, and take a ritualistic dip, believing that it bestows intellectual brilliance, artistic talents, and refined character

5. Maghi Purnima (February 12th, 2025) – The Day of Charity

Maghi Purnima is a sacred day of spiritual reflection, generosity, and meditation. Devotees are encouraged to engage in charitable acts, as it is believed that donations made on this day return manifold as divine blessings. Bathing at the Sangam during Maghi Purnima is said to cleanse one's soul and align them with the path of Dharma (righteousness)

6. Maha Shivratri (February 26th, 2025) – The Final Amrit Snan

Maha Shivratri, known as the "Great Night of Lord Shiva," marks the culmination of the Maha Kumbh Mela. It is believed to be the most spiritually charged night, where devotees seek inner transformation and detachment from material desires. Bathing on this day is considered a gateway to divine consciousness, helping devotees shed ignorance and embrace the wisdom of Lord Shiva

Astrological and Spiritual Significance

Each Amrit Snan (Shahi Snan) is meticulously scheduled based on planetary configurations, particularly the positions of the Sun, Moon, and Jupiter. These celestial alignments are believed to heighten the spiritual energy of the sacred waters, making them exceptionally powerful for cleansing karmic debts and attaining spiritual elevation.

Bathing at the Triveni Sangam during these auspicious days is considered a soul-liberating experience, aligning an individual's inner energies with the cosmic forces. Devotees believe that immersing themselves in these holy waters helps them shed past burdens, embrace enlightenment, and progress toward Moksha (liberation).

The Maha Kumbh Mela 2025 is not just a pilgrimage—it is a spiritual confluence where faith, devotion, and cosmic energies unite, offering millions the opportunity to experience divine transformation.

Benefits

Taking a dip during Amrit Snan (Shahi Snan) is thought to:

- Cleanses sins: Purifies the soul and removes past karmic debts
- Spiritual liberation: Helps in attaining Moksha
- Emotional and physical well-being: Reduces stress and anxiety

Attendance at Maha Kumbh Mela 2025

The Maha Kumbh Mela 2025 has witnessed an unprecedented turnout, with over 650+ million devotees participating in the holy dip at Triveni Sangam. On January 29th, 2025, during the Mauni Amavasya Amrit Snan (Shahi Snan), approximately 57 million pilgrims gathered, marking one of the largest single-day congregations. Despite challenges, including a tragic stampede on the most auspicious day, the festival draws millions, underscoring its profound spiritual significance.

In essence, the Amrit Snan during the Maha Kumbh Mela serves as a powerful testament to millions' enduring faith and devotion, offering a unique opportunity for spiritual cleansing and renewal in alignment with cosmic forces.

People from all parts of the world, irrespective of religion, caste, or belief, came to the holy Triveni Sangam to witness the once-in-a-lifetime event and participate in the biggest human gathering in mankind's history.

The Maha Kumbh Mela has consistently drawn vast numbers of devotees, with attendance figures showcasing a remarkable upward trajectory over the years. In 2013, the festival witnessed approximately 30 million participants. This number saw a significant increase during the 2019 Ardh Kumbh Mela, attracting around 50 million attendees. The 2025 Maha Kumbh Mela has set unprecedented records, with over 650 million devotees, solidifying its status as the largest human gathering in recorded history.

This exponential growth in attendance underscores the enduring spiritual significance of the Maha Kumbh Mela and reflects the increasing devotion among participants worldwide.

This year's figure not only surpasses previous records but also highlights the event's growing significance and the enhanced capacity to accommodate such massive gatherings. The festival's success reflects meticulous planning, infrastructural developments, and the unwavering faith of millions who journey to the sacred Triveni Sangam (confluence of the Ganges, Yamuna, and Saraswati rivers).

Year	Estimated Attendance	Notes
1954	Approximately 5 million	Marked by a tragic stampede resulting in numerous fatalities
1977	Around 15 million	Significant increase in participation
1989	Approximately 30 million	Continued growth in pilgrim numbers.
2013	About 120 million	One of the largest gatherings, with over 30 million on a single day
2025	Surpassed 650+ million	Record-breaking turnout, with 650+ million by the festival's conclusion

The Akharas

The Akharas are monastic orders of sadhus (ascetics) that play a central role in the Kumbh Mela.

The Akharas are monastic orders of ascetics in Sanatan/Hinduism, playing a pivotal role in preserving and propagating spiritual traditions. They are primarily categorized based on their devotion to specific deities and philosophical schools, namely -

- Shaiva (followers of Lord Shiva)
- Vaishnava (followers of Lord Vishnu)
- Udasin (neutral or renunciant sects)

Each Akhara has a distinct lineage, philosophy, and function within the religious ecosystem of Bharat.

Below is a detailed overview of the prominent Akharas, including their founding details, significance, headquarters, main deity, speciality, and sect affiliation.

List of Prominent Akharas and Their Details

Role of Akharas in Kumbh Mela

The Akharas are the spiritual and organizational backbone of the Kumbh Mela. They lead the Amrit Snan (Shahi Snan), marking the beginning of each bathing ritual. The sequence in which different Akharas enter the Sangam is determined by ancient traditions, with Shaiva Akharas usually leading the procession.

Shaiva Akharas (Followers of Lord Shiva)

Shaiva Akharas primarily consist of Naga Sadhus, known for their renunciation and intense meditation practices. They are the first to take the Amrit Snan (Shahi Snan) at Kumbh Mela.

Juna Akhara

- **Founded:** 4th Century CE (by Adi Shankaracharya)

- **Significance:** Largest and oldest Akhara, known for its warrior ascetics and strict discipline

- **Headquarters:** Varanasi, Uttar Pradesh

- **Main Deity:** Lord Dattatreya (incarnation of Lord Vishnu)

- **Specialty:** Home to Naga Sadhus, who remain naked and covered in ash, practicing extreme renunciation

Mahanirvani Akhara

- **Founded:** 8th Century CE

- **Significance:** Among the most powerful Akharas, closely associated with Advaita Vedanta and Tantra

- **Headquarters:** Prayagraj, Uttar Pradesh

- **Main Deity:** Lord Shiva

- **Specialty:** It traditionally leads the first procession at Kumbh Mela

Atal Akhara

- **Founded:** 646 CE

- **Significance:** Balances Bhakti (devotion) and Tapasya (austerity)

- **Headquarters:** Varanasi, Uttar Pradesh

- **Main Deity:** Lord Shiva

- **Specialty:** Known for deep spiritual knowledge and preserving ancient Hindu texts

Niranjani Akhara

- **Founded:** 904 CE

- **Significance:** One of the most influential Akharas, known for intellectual prowess and spiritual discipline

- **Headquarters:** Prayagraj, Uttar Pradesh

- **Main Deity:** Lord Shiva

- **Specialty:** Holds high political and spiritual influence within the Kumbh Mela. Unlike Juna Akhara, Niranjani Akhara members are not strictly Naga Sadhus; they include Dandi Sannyasis (staff-bearing monks). Maintains a strict hierarchy and disciplinary code

Avahan Akhara

- **Founded:** 6th Century CE

- **Significance:** One of the strongest warriors Akharas, focuses on asceticism and defense

- **Headquarters:** Haridwar, Uttarakhand

- **Main Deity:** Lord Shiva

- **Specialty:** Its Naga Sadhus are known for their fearlessness and physical endurance

Agni Akhara

- **Founded:** 8th Century CE (Revived in the 18th century)

- **Significance:** One of the oldest but less dominant Akharas

- **Headquarters:** Nasik, Maharashtra

- **Main Deity:** Lord Shiva

- **Specialty:** Known as the "Warrior Akhara", historically training its sadhus in martial arts and weapons. Closely linked with the Shaivite military traditions. Plays an active role in the Amrit Snan (Shahi Snan) processions during Kumbh Mela

Anand Akhara

- **Founded:** 13th Century CE

- **Significance:** Smallest Shaiva Akhara, following strict ascetic traditions

- **Headquarters:** Varanasi, Uttar Pradesh

- **Main Deity:** Lord Shiva

- **Specialty:** Focuses on meditation, yoga, and self-discipline

Vaishnava Akharas (Followers of Lord Vishnu): These Akharas consist of Bairagi (mendicant monks) devoted to Lord Vishnu and his avatars (Rama & Krishna).

Nirvani Ani Akhara

- **Founded:** 16th Century CE

- **Significance:** Most powerful Vaishnava Akhara, deeply involved in the Ram Janmabhoomi movement

- **Headquarters:** Ayodhya, Uttar Pradesh

- **Main Deity:** Lord Vishnu (Rama)

- **Specialty:** Known for its scriptural knowledge and temple preservation efforts

Nirmohi Ani Akhara

- **Founded:** 18th Century CE

- **Significance:** Dedicated exclusively to the worship of Lord Rama

- **Headquarters:** Ayodhya, Uttar Pradesh

- **Main Deity:** Lord Vishnu (Rama)

- **Specialty:** Engaged in preserving ancient Hindu traditions and running ashrams

Digambar Ani Akhara

- **Founded:** 18th Century CE

- **Significance:** One of the main Vaishnava ascetic orders, focusing on spiritual knowledge

- **Headquarters:** Nashik, Maharashtra

- **Main Deity:** Lord Vishnu

- **Specialty:** The monks wear saffron robes (unlike Shaiva Naga Sadhus) and focus on Vaishnava scriptures

Udasin Akharas (Neutral or Renunciant Sects): Udasin Akharas are non-sectarian and do not strictly follow Shaivism or Vaishnavism. They originated from Guru Nanak's disciple, Baba Sri Chand.

Udasin Panchayati Akhara

- **Founded:** 17th Century CE

- **Significance:** Established by Guru Nanak's followers under Baba Sri Chand's guidance

- **Headquarters:** Haridwar, Uttarakhand

- **Main Deity:** Lord Shiva and Vishnu

- **Specialty:** Blends Hindu and Sikh traditions, promoting yoga, meditation, and Vedanta philosophy

Naya Udasin Akhara

- **Founded:** 18th Century CE

- **Significance:** A newer branch of the Udasin sect, following strict renunciation

- **Headquarters:** Punjab

- **Main Deity:** Lord Shiva and Vishnu

- **Specialty:** Encourages scriptural study and ascetic living. Ensures discipline and organization among Vaishnava monks. Often acts as an umbrella body for Vaishnava sects, resolving disputes. Plays a major role in temple administration and religious discourses

Other (Unique) Akharas

This category includes non-traditional Akharas that do not strictly follow the Shaiva or Vaishnava sects.

Kinnar Akhara

- **Founded:** 2015 CE (Modern Formation)

- **Significance:** The first-ever Akhara for the transgender community (Kinnars/Third Gender)

- **Headquarters:** Prayagraj, Uttar Pradesh

- **Main Deity:** Goddess Bahuchara Mata (Goddess of Transgender Community)

- **Specialty:** Founded by Mahamandaleshwar Laxmi Narayan Tripathi, a renowned transgender activist. Challenges the traditional exclusion of Kinnars from Hindu spiritual leadership. Actively participates in the Amrit Snan (Shahi

Snan) processions, though they are not recognized by other mainstream Akharas

Role of Akharas in Kumbh Mela

The Akharas are the spiritual and organizational backbone of the Kumbh Mela. They lead the Amrit Snan (Shahi Snan), marking the beginning of each bathing ritual. The sequence in which different Akharas enter the Sangam is determined by ancient traditions, with Shaiva Akharas usually leading the procession.

Significance of This Sequence in Kumbh Mela

1. Shaiva Akharas (Naga Sadhus) go first because they are considered the warrior monks and defenders of the Sanatan Dharma

2. Vaishnava Akharas (Bairagi Sadhus) follow next, representing the path of devotion and spiritual enlightenment

3. Udasin Akharas come later, as they are neutral and focus on a blend of Shaivism & Vaishnavism

4. Kinnar Akhara, the newest addition, takes its place at the end, symbolizing inclusivity and change in modern Hinduism

Significance of Akharas in Society

1. **Spiritual Guardians**: Preserve and promote Hindu philosophical traditions

2. **Social Reformers**: Many Akharas engage in humanitarian work like running ashrams and schools

3. **Defenders of Dharma**: Historically, Akharas maintained military units to protect temples from invaders

The Akharas have played a pivotal role in shaping Hindu religious traditions for centuries. Their influence continues to grow as millions of devotees seek guidance from these ascetics during events like the Maha Kumbh Mela. With their rich history, deep spiritual wisdom, and dedication to dharma, the Akharas remain guardians of Bharat's sacred traditions and cultural heritage.

Places to visit at

MahaKumbh & Prayagraj –

Spiritual, Cultural & Technological Experience

🌿 Plan your journey, embrace the divine, and witness history in the making. 🌿

The MahaKumbh 2025 in Prayagraj is a remarkable convergence that encapsulates the essence of Bharat's rich legacy, historical depth, and unwavering devotion. As Teerthraj Prayag, this sacred city serves as a cornerstone of spiritual insight, cultural splendor, and modern technological innovation.

Here's a detailed exploration of the must-visit places and experiences during MahaKumbh and after -

Triveni Sangam / Sangam Nose – The Divine Confluence

- **Location:** Convergence of Ganga, Yamuna, and the spiritual Saraswati
- **Historical & Scriptural Significance:**

  o The Vedas and Puranas describe Triveni Sangam as the holiest site for purification and attaining Moksha

  o In the Ramayana, Lord Rama visited this sacred spot during his exile

- o In the Mahabharata, the Pandavas performed rituals here before their final journey

- **This is a permanent place and mostly open for people the entire year**

  - o The Amrit Snan by Akharas takes place here

  - o A dip in the Sangam is believed to cleanse sins and grant salvation

  - o Experience the majestic sunrise and evening Aarti on boats

Bade Hanuman Ji – The Reclining Deity

- **Location:** Near the Sangam, inside the Prayagraj Fort
- **Historical & Scriptural Significance:**

  - o The only reclining idol of Lord Hanuman, measuring over 20 feet in length

  - o During floods, the rising waters of the Ganga are believed to touch Hanuman's feet as an offering of devotion

  - o The Lete Hanuman Ji Temple, holds immense spiritual significance. This unique posture symbolizes rest after completing divine tasks

- This is a permanent place and one of the major attractions of Prayagraj

- Devotees believe that praying here removes obstacles and grants strength

- The temple is a major attraction during Kumbh Mela

Akshay Vat – The Eternal Banyan Tree

- **Location:** Inside Prayagraj Fort, near Patalpuri Temple
- **Historical & Scriptural Significance:**

  - Mentioned in the Ramayana and Mahabharata, this tree is said to be indestructible/symbol of immortality

  - Lord Rama, Sita, and Lakshman are believed to have visited here

  - The Puranas state that even during Pralaya (the great deluge), Akshay Vat remained standing

  - The Akshay Vat or "Indestructible Banyan Tree" is an ancient fig tree symbolizing eternal life and resilience. It is believed to have witnessed countless ages

- A sacred site for meditation and offering prayers

- Its divine aura makes it a must-visit for seekers of spiritual enlightenment

Alopi Maa Mandir – The Unique Shaktipeeth

- **Location:** Near Alopibagh, Prayagraj
- **Historical & Scriptural Significance:**

  - It is believed to be the spot where Maa Sati's last body part (or energy) disappeared, making it a revered Shaktipeeth

  - The temple does not have a traditional idol but a sacred wooden platform representing divine energy

- Situated near the bank of river Ganga

- Devotees visit to seek protection and strength from the Goddess

- The temple comes alive during Navratri and Kumbh Mela

Lalita Devi Mandir – The Powerful Shaktipeeth

- **Location: Meerapur, Prayagraj**
- **Historical & Scriptural Significance:**

  - Considered one of the 51 Shaktipeeths, dedicated to Goddess Lalita, a form of Parvati

  - Associated with Devi Sati's fingers falling here, as per ancient scriptures

- Situated near the bank of river Yamuna. it is revered in ancient texts as a manifestation of divine feminine power. A must-visit for divine blessings and spiritual awakening

Naag Vasuki Mandir – The Temple of the Serpent King

Location: Daraganj, Prayagraj

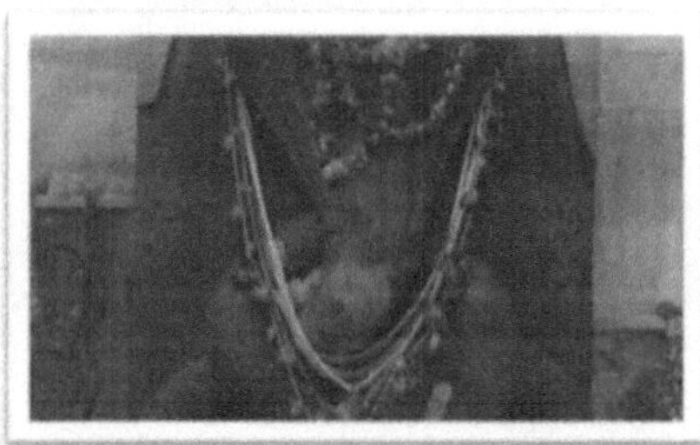

- **Historical & Scriptural Significance:**

  - Dedicated to Naag Vasuki, the divine serpent associated with Samudra Manthan

- o The temple is mentioned in Skanda Purana as an important site for Naga worship

- o The king of serpents, revered for protection and overcoming adversities

- The temple is especially significant during Nag Panchami

- Devotees believe that worshipping here removes Kaal Sarp Dosha

Nishad Raj Park – Honoring an Ancient Friendship of Lord Rama and Nishadraj

- **Location:** Shringverpur Dham, Prayagraj
- **Historical & Scriptural Significance:**

- o Dedicated to Nishad Raj Guhya, the king of boatmen who helped Lord Rama cross the Ganga river during exile

- o Celebrates the bond of friendship between Nishad Raj and Lord Rama

- o Shringverpur is named after the Spiritual Saint Shringi Rishis

- A serene park with statues and murals depicting Ramayana episodes

- A perfect place for reflection and historical appreciation

Bharadwaj Muni Ashram – The Seat of Knowledge

- **Location:** Colonelganj Road, Prayagraj
- **Historical & Scriptural Significance:**

  - The great sage Maharishi Bharadwaj, one of the Sapta Rishis, meditated and taught students here

  - According to the Ramayana, Lord Rama visited this Ashram during his exile and sought Maharishi Bharadwaj's blessings

  - The Mahabharata also mentions this Ashram as a center of Vedic learning

- Experience a divine atmosphere of learning and meditation

- A place where seekers of wisdom, Vedic knowledge, and spirituality gather

Boat Club – The Gateway to Sangam

- **Location:** Near Saraswati Ghat, Prayagraj
- **Significance:**

    o The primary point for boat rides to the Sangam

    o A great way to enjoy the sunrise and evening Aarti on the river

- Experience the tranquillity of the holy rivers

- Perfect for photography and serene reflections

Spectacular Shows at MahaKumbh 2025

1. Laser Show – A Divine Visual Experience

Location: Banks of Ganga, Near Sangam

- Themes: Stories from Ramayana, Mahabharata, and Kumbh Mela's history

- This is a short-duration show and in this a mesmerizing light & sound spectacle illuminating the night sky

2. Drone Show – Celestial Choreography

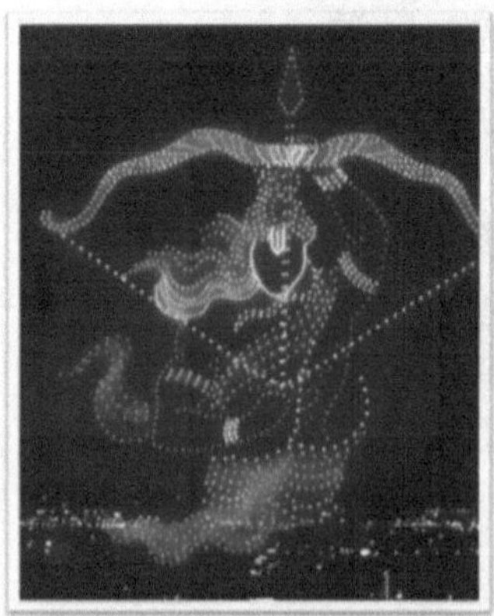

Location: Kumbh Mela Grounds

- Themes: Spiritual symbols, Indian heritage, and ancient scriptures

- A stunning digital tribute to faith and tradition that has been organized for a shorter duration during the MahaKumbh

3. Shivalaya Park, located in Arail near Triveni Pushp in Prayagraj,

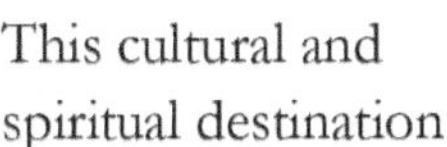

It spans approximately 12 acres and is uniquely designed to mirror the map of India.

This cultural and spiritual destination

features replicas of prominent temples, including the 12 Jyotirlingas, positioned according to their actual geographical locations, offering visitors a virtual pilgrimage experience.

The park also showcases art, culture, and civilization from various states and union territories, enhancing its significance as a center for cultural unity and spiritual enrichment.

A Journey of Faith, Culture & Technology

The Mahakumbh 2025 in Prayagraj is not just a pilgrimage; it's a grand confluence of devotion, history, and modernity. Whether you seek spiritual upliftment, cultural enlightenment, or a technological marvel, Mahakumbh has something for everyone.

Digital MahaKumbh

The Maha Kumbh Mela 2025 in Prayagraj stands as a monumental testament to Bharat's spiritual heritage, drawing an unprecedented gathering of devotees from across the globe. This event, occurring once every 144 years, has prompted extensive preparations, infrastructural developments, and meticulous planning to accommodate the massive influx of pilgrims. This massive religious gathering drawn around 650+ million devotees over 45 days from 13th January to 26 February, 2025.

Here's a detailed look at the preparations, budget, city changes, transformations, arrangements, administrative setup, security, and transportation:

Budget and Economic Impact

The Uttar Pradesh government, in collaboration with central agencies, has allocated approximately **Rs.12,670 crore** for the Maha Kumbh 2025. This substantial investment aims to ensure a seamless

experience for all attendees. The event is projected to generate up to Rs.2 lakh crore in economic growth for the state, significantly boosting local businesses and tourism sectors.

Infrastructure Developments: City Changes and Transformations

Prayagraj has undergone significant transformations to host the Mahakumbh. To accommodate the vast number of pilgrims, a temporary city spanning 4,000 hectares has been established. The city has seen the construction of temporary shelters, food stalls, sanitation facilities, and emergency medical services.

The Prayagraj Airport has been expanded to handle the increased passenger volume, with records showing over 100 flights handled in a single day. Roads leading to Prayagraj have been upgraded, and a "No Vehicle" zone has been implemented in the Kumbh area to manage traffic.

Key infrastructural enhancements include:

Roads and Bridges: Renovation of 92 roads and beautification of 17 major routes. Construction of 30 pontoon bridges using 3,308 pontoons

Accommodation: Erection of 150,000 tents to house pilgrims, with options ranging from basic shelters to luxury accommodations

Sanitation: Installation of over 150,000 toilets and urinals, maintained by a dedicated team of 10,000+ sanitation workers

Grand Arrangements at Mahakumbh 2025: Food, Accommodation, & Sanitation for Pilgrims

The Mahakumbh 2025 in Prayagraj is the largest human gathering on Earth, drawing an estimated 650+ million pilgrims worldwide. Ensuring smooth operations for such an enormous crowd requires meticulous planning, state-of-the-art infrastructure, and an unwavering commitment to hospitality and hygiene.

The arrangements for food, accommodation, and sanitation reflect the efficiency of modern administration and the essence of Bharat's spiritual and cultural ethos.

Food Arrangements: Nourishment for the Soul and Body

Providing food for half a billion visitors is an enormous task, but MahaKumbh 2025 rises to the challenge with Langars (community kitchens), street food  stalls, and local eateries, ensuring that no one goes hungry.

- **Langars: Free Community Kitchens Serving Millions**

  - Organized by spiritual organizations, temples, and charitable trusts, Langars operate 24/7 to serve fresh, hot meals to devotees

  - Offerings include Khichdi, Puri-Sabzi, Dal-Roti, Chai, and seasonal fruits, ensuring simple yet nutritious meals

o Run entirely by volunteers (Sevadars) who selflessly serve food as an act of devotion

- **Local Street Food Delights**

For those looking to explore the culinary richness of Prayagraj, Mahakumbh offers an array of street food options, blending tradition and flavors:

o Chaat (Aloo Tikki, Papdi Chaat, Dahi Bhalla) – A burst of tangy and spicy flavors

o Bedai-Kachori with Aloo Sabzi – A local breakfast staple

o Lassi and Thandai – Refreshing and rich, made from yogurt, nuts, and saffron

o Malaiyyo – A winter specialty, an ethereal, saffron-infused milk froth

- **Shops & Restaurants for Diverse Needs**

o Vegetarian food stalls dominate, in line with spiritual traditions, ensuring purity in preparation

o Special arrangements for international pilgrims, including Jain, South Indian, and Continental meals at designated food hubs

o Hygienic packaged food stations for visitors preferring quick, on-the-go options

- **Advanced Food Safety Measures**

  - AI-powered food safety monitoring ensures hygiene and quality standards

  - Real-time tracking of food distribution prevents shortages

  - 24/7 health inspections ensure adherence to safety protocols

Accommodation: From Tents to Luxury Stays

MahaKumbh 2025 offers a wide variety of staying options, ranging from free campsites to high-end hotels, ensuring every visitor finds suitable lodging.

- **Tent Cities: The Spiritual Retreat**

  - Lakhs of tents have been set up across designated zones, categorized into basic, deluxe, and premium

  - Ashrams and religious sects provide free stay options with bedding, meals, and spiritual discourses

  - Eco-friendly accommodations made from sustainable materials promote environmental consciousness

- **Hotels & Guesthouses for Comfort Seekers**

  o Government and private hotels have been booked in advance to cater to international visitors and dignitaries

  o Luxury stays with modern amenities, offering Wi-Fi, 24-hour security, and guided tours

- **Dharamshalas & Ashrams: A Spiritual Experience**

  o Several age-old Ashrams and Dharamshalas provide free or budget-friendly lodging to pilgrims

  o Many Ashrams also conduct daily discourses, meditation sessions, and community meals

- **Digital Booking & Smart Allocation**

  o The Kumbh Mela online portal and mobile apps allow pilgrims to pre-book accommodations

  o AI-based allocation ensures equal distribution and prevents overcrowding

Sanitation & Hygiene: World-Class Infrastructure

Maintaining cleanliness for such a vast population requires state-of-the-art sanitation facilities and strict hygiene protocols.

Smart Public Toilets: A Hygiene Revolution

- o Over 100,000 eco-friendly, biotilets installed across the Kumbh area

- o Automated cleaning systems ensure regular sanitation

- o Separate facilities for men, women, children, and specially-abled individuals

- **Bathing & Changing Zones**

- o Dedicated bathing ghats with temporary changing rooms for comfort

- o Separate bathing slots for Akharas, pilgrims, and international visitors to ensure smooth flow

- o Deploy lifeguards and medical teams at key bathing spots

Waste Management & Environmental Initiatives

- o Zero-waste policy: Extensive use of biodegradable utensils, waste segregation, and recycling units

- o Massive cleanliness drives led by Swachh Bharat Mission volunteers

- o AI-monitored waste disposal to maintain sanitation standards

- **Tech-Driven Sanitation Monitoring**

  - IoT-enabled smart toilets track cleanliness levels

  - Drones and CCTV monitoring ensure real-time sanitation updates

  - Mobile sanitation apps allow visitors to locate nearest clean washrooms

Arrangements and Administrative Setup

The administrative arrangements for the MahaKumbh are extensive. The Uttar Pradesh government has deployed thousands of volunteers, security personnel, and medical teams to ensure the safety and convenience of the visitors. The city has been divided into various zones, each managed by a dedicated team of officials. The government has also set up a Climate awareness forum and Bird Festival to promote environmental conservation during the event.

Technological and Security Measures

Security is a top priority for Mahakumbh 2025. The Uttar Pradesh government has extended the duties of police personnel and officials to manage the large crowds. A comprehensive security plan has been put in place, including the deployment of CCTV cameras, metal detectors, and regular patrolling by security forces. The city has been divided into multiple security zones, each monitored by a dedicated team of officers. Over 37,000 police officers were transferred to Prayagraj from other cities to manage the event.

Ensuring the safety and convenience of pilgrims is paramount. Measures implemented include:

Surveillance: Managing such a vast congregation posed significant challenges, particularly concerning crowd control and preventing stampedes. To address these, over 2,700 AI-enabled CCTV cameras were strategically installed across the festival grounds. These cameras, integrated with AI-based software, monitored crowd density in real time, identifying potential congestion points and alerting authorities to unusual activities. This proactive approach allowed for timely interventions, significantly reducing the risk of accidents

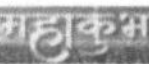

Facial Recognition for Reuniting Families: The vastness of the event often led to individuals, including children and the elderly, getting separated from their groups. To combat this, facial recognition technology was employed to swiftly locate and reunite missing persons. More than 20,000 people were united using this technology

Integration of Drones and Underwater Surveillance: Enhancing the technological framework, drones equipped with AI capabilities provided aerial surveillance, offering real-time data on crowd movements and identifying potential hazards from above. Additionally, underwater drones monitored the depths of the confluence where pilgrims took their holy dips, ensuring immediate response to any incidents of drowning or water-related accidents.

Multilingual Chatbots and Mobile Applications: To assist the diverse populace attending the Mela, multilingual AI-powered chatbots were integrated into the official Kumbh Mela mobile application. These chatbots provided real-time information, answered queries in multiple languages, and guided pilgrims through the vast festival area, enhancing their overall experience

Enhanced Security Measures: The fusion of AI and facial recognition extended to security protocols. The AI-driven systems could detect unauthorized access, identify suspicious activities, and promptly alert security personnel, thereby bolstering the safety of attendees. This technological vigilance ensured that potential threats were addressed swiftly, maintaining the sanctity and security of the event

Medical Facilities: Establishment of temporary hospitals equipped with surgical and diagnostic services, alongside mobile health units and emergency medical services

Fire Safety: Allocation of Rs.131.48 crores for fire safety, including the deployment of 4 Articulating Water Towers, 351 firefighting vehicles, and 50+ fire stations that were capable of addressing fires up to 35 meters high

The successful implementation of these technologies at the Maha Kumbh Mela 2025 not only ensured the safety and well-being of

millions but also set a precedent for managing large-scale events worldwide through the integration of AI and advanced surveillance systems.

Transportation

To efficiently manage the massive influx of pilgrims attending MahaKumbh 2025, extensive transportation arrangements have been implemented. The Prayagraj Airport has undergone significant

expansion to accommodate the surge in air travelers, with infrastructure upgrades enabling the airport to handle over 100 flights in a single day, a record-breaking capacity for the region.

Road Infrastructure & Traffic Management

Recognizing the immense vehicular pressure, major roads leading to Prayagraj have been widened, with several single-lane roads expanded into two to four lanes to facilitate smoother traffic movement. Additionally, new flyovers and bypasses have been constructed to reduce congestion at critical junctions.

To decongest the city center, a "No Vehicle Zone" has been designated in and around the Kumbh Mela premises, ensuring pedestrian safety and smoother movement for emergency services. Authorities have also urged local residents to minimize the use of four-wheelers during peak pilgrimage days, encouraging the use of public transportation and shared mobility options instead.

Public Transport Augmentation

To support the increased demand, special trains and buses have been deployed, connecting Prayagraj to key cities across India. Railway stations have been upgraded with additional  ticket counters, waiting areas, and security checkpoints to streamline passenger flow. State-run and private bus services have increased their fleet, offering frequent shuttle services from designated transit hubs to the Kumbh area.

Additionally, water transport options have been introduced along the Yamuna and Ganga rivers, providing an alternative means of travel while reducing road congestion. Digital signage and real-time traffic monitoring using AI-based surveillance systems are also being utilized to make dynamic route adjustments, ensuring efficient crowd movement throughout the event.

These proactive transportation and infrastructure measures have been instrumental in transforming Prayagraj into a well-coordinated pilgrimage hub, showcasing the city's ability to handle one of the world's largest human congregations with precision and efficiency.

City Transformation and Cultural Initiatives

Prayagraj has undergone significant transformations to enhance the pilgrim experience:

Urban Beautification: Extensive wall paintings and murals depicting episodes from religious scriptures and folklore adorn the city

Cultural Events: Daily performances by renowned artists, poets, and classical musicians celebrate India's rich cultural tapestry

The Maha Kumbh Mela 2025 exemplifies a harmonious blend of tradition and modernity. Through meticulous planning, substantial investments, and a commitment to preserving cultural heritage, Prayagraj is poised to host a transformative, spiritually enriching and logistically seamless event for millions of devotees worldwide. The extensive preparations and arrangements reflect the government's

commitment to ensuring a safe and memorable event for all participants.

It is right to call the Maha Kumbh 2025 a "Digital MahaKumbh" due to the widespread integration of  advanced technologies that enhance the spiritual, logistical, and security aspects of the event. With AI-powered surveillance, drone monitoring, cashless transactions, digital crowd management, and real-time information through mobile apps, the event showcases Bharat's (India) technological prowess and digital readiness on a global scale.

The use of QR-coded passes, virtual pilgrim assistance, and AI-driven traffic control ensure seamless crowd movement, reflecting the nation's rapid progress in smart governance and digital transformation. This evolution of Kumbh from a purely traditional gathering to a high-tech, well-orchestrated digital experience symbolizes not just the advancement of human civilization but also Bharat's emergence as a leader in digital innovation, seamlessly blending ancient wisdom with modern technology to create an unparalleled spiritual and technological confluence.

The Perfect Balance of Tradition and Modernity

The arrangements at MahaKumbh 2025 reflect Bharat's commitment to both tradition and progress. From massive food distribution to high-tech sanitation solutions, every aspect has been meticulously planned to accommodate half a billion visitors while upholding spiritual values.

The event is a testament to human coordination, technological advancement, and the timeless hospitality of Bharat.

As pilgrims gather to seek spiritual enlightenment, they also witness a logistical marvel that redefines the possibilities of mass gatherings.

'जाकी रही भावना जैसी, प्रभु मूरत देखी तिन तैसी'

इसका मतलब है कि जिसकी जैसी भावना होती है,

उसे वैसा ही परिणाम मिलता है.

यह कथन रामचरित मानस की चौपाई से लिया गया है।

Jaaki rahi bhavana jaise, Prabhu murat dekhi tin taisi'

This means that one who has similar feelings,

He gets the same result.

This statement has been taken from Chaupai of Ramcharit Manas!

Digital Integration and Management
-

Innovative Transformations: Bridging Tradition with Modern Technology at MahaKumbh 2025

Management Excellence

MahaKumbh 2025 is not just the largest religious congregation in the world; it is also an extraordinary Use Case for management professionals, showcasing an intricate blend of tradition, modern technology, and meticulous event planning. Beyond its spiritual, cultural, and scientific significance, this massive event exemplifies advancements in Digitalization, Artificial Intelligence, Program Management, Lean Six Sigma, Data Science, and Event & Business Management principles.

Understanding Perception: A Management Perspective

In any large-scale event, perception plays a vital role. People see and interpret based on their field of expertise and interest.

This is similar to the incident from the Mahabharata, where Guru Dronacharya asked his students what they observed when looking at a tree. While most students described the tree, bird, and sky, Arjun, as an expert archer, focused solely on the eye of the bird.

Similarly, MahaKumbh 2025 presents multiple perspectives:

- Spiritual seekers observe Saints, Gurus, and rituals

- Environmentalists analyze water quality and pollution control measures

- Entrepreneurs identify business opportunities

- Social media influencers document content for digital platforms

- Civic authorities monitor infrastructure and sanitation challenges

- Management professionals, however, witness an extraordinary demonstration of program governance, scope management, data analytics, risk mitigation, and quality control

Transformation and Digital Evolution

The MahaKumbh 2025 has embraced digital & non-digital transformation to enhance the pilgrim experience. The implementation of the Digital MahaKumbh initiative has introduced virtual guidance, informational apps, interactive kiosks, and augmented reality experiences. This integration of technology ensures that pilgrims are well-informed and can navigate the event seamlessly, thereby enhancing overall satisfaction and safety.

MahaKumbh 2025 exemplifies Transformation at multiple levels:

1. **Physical Infrastructure:** Upgraded roads, temporary housing, sanitation facilities, and optimized traffic management

2. **Digital Integration:** Smart surveillance, facial recognition for security, real-time monitoring, and AI-driven crowd management

3. **Automation & AI:** Predictive analytics for crowd control, **RFID-based tracking** for lost individuals, and AI-driven chatbot assistance

4. **Sustainability Measures:** Waste management strategies, water conservation, and solar-powered infrastructure

The digital footprint of the event is unprecedented, making it a Digital MahaKumbh, showcasing Bharat's advancements in smart governance and event technology. The MahaKumbh 2025 in Prayagraj stands as a monumental testament to Bharat's commitment to seamlessly blending tradition with modernity. This event has catalyzed transformative developments across Bharat (India), Uttar Pradesh (UP), and Prayagraj, encompassing infrastructure, technology, and cultural heritage.

National Transformation: Bharat's Technological and Cultural Renaissance

1. Infrastructure Development

- **Ganga Expressway**: Spanning approximately 594 kilometers, this expressway connects Meerut to Prayagraj, significantly reducing travel time and enhancing regional connectivity. The project, with an estimated cost of Rs.36,230 crores, was fast-tracked to facilitate pilgrim movement during Mahakumbh 2025

2. Digital Integration

- **Artificial Intelligence (AI) and Surveillance**: To manage the anticipated influx of over 650+ million devotees, AI-powered cameras and drones have been deployed for real-

time crowd monitoring, ensuring safety and efficient crowd control

- **Digital Payment Ecosystem**: Embracing a cashless economy, major transactions during the event were conducted digitally, showcasing India's advancements in financial technology

City-Level Advancements: Uttar Pradesh's Strategic Initiatives

Architectural and Civil Engineering Marvel

The architectural planning for the MahaKumbh encompasses civil, digital, and technical aspects. The layout includes well-designed infrastructure such as temporary shelters, sanitation facilities, food stalls, and emergency services. The design ensures optimal utilization of space and resources, accommodating the influx of millions of pilgrims without compromising on safety and convenience.

The city of Prayagraj has undergone a significant transformation to accommodate over 650+ million visitors:

- Temporary bridges constructed over the Ganga and Yamuna for efficient movement

- Massive tent cities designed for pilgrims, ensuring safety, hygiene, and comfort

- Emergency evacuation zones strategically placed for quick response

- Waste disposal and water treatment plants set up to minimize ecological impact

1. Infrastructure Enhancements

- **Road and Bridge Projects**: The city has initiated a comprehensive renovation of 92 roads and has beautified 17 major routes. To ensure seamless travel for pilgrims, 30 pontoon bridges have been constructed

- **Transportation Facilities**: The introduction of new bus stations and the expansion of railway services, including special trains, have been implemented to accommodate the massive influx of visitors from all over the country

- **Expansion of Lanes**: Several single-lane roads have been upgraded to 2 to 4 lanes, effectively doubling or quadrupling their capacity to handle vehicular traffic. This expansion is crucial for managing the expected surge during the MahaKumbh

2. Security Measures

- Enhanced Surveillance: Deployment of 2,750 AI-based CCTV cameras and a security force comprising 37,000 policemen and 14,000 home guards ensure a safe environment for all attendees

3. Elevated Corridor: Airport to High Court

- **Construction of Elevated Road**: A pivotal project is the construction of an elevated road connecting Prayagraj Airport to the Allahabad High Court. This overpass, extending approximately 2 kilometers, is designed to provide a direct and congestion-free route for commuters

- **Decongestion of Surface Roads**: By diverting a substantial volume of traffic above ground, surface roads experience less congestion, leading to smoother traffic flow

- **Enhanced Safety**: Elevated roads minimize points of conflict between vehicles and pedestrians, thereby reducing the likelihood of accidents

Local Developments: Transforming Prayagraj

1. Urban Planning and Infrastructure

- **Temporary City Setup**: MahaKumbh Nagar has been established, featuring thousands of tents and shelters, including luxury accommodations like the IRCTC's "MahaKumbh Gram," offering modern amenities to visitors

- **Sanitation and Cleanliness**: Over 150,000 toilets have been installed, and maintained by a dedicated workforce of 10,000+ sanitation workers, ensuring hygiene and cleanliness throughout the event

2. Cultural and Technological Integration

- **Incredible Bharat (India) Pavilion:** The Ministry of Tourism has established this pavilion to provide information and engage tourists, media, and influencers, promoting Bharat's rich cultural heritage

- **Kalagram Cultural Village**: This cultural hub features performances, traditional crafts, and culinary experiences, offering visitors an immersive experience of Bharat's diverse traditions

These infrastructural advancements not only aim to facilitate the movement of pilgrims during the MahaKumbh but also promise long-term benefits for the residents of Prayagraj. The strategic expansion and modernization of the city's road network are poised to bolster economic activities, improve daily commutes, and

elevate the overall quality of urban life.

The MahaKumbh 2025 exemplifies a harmonious fusion of spirituality, culture, and technological innovation, positioning Bharat as a global leader in orchestrating large-scale events with precision and cultural depth.

Event Planning & Scope Management

Planning the MahaKumbh involves a high level of coordination and communication among numerous stakeholders.

From setting up the Tent City to organizing the Laser and Drone Shows, every aspect is meticulously planned. Event planners employ Value Stream Mapping to streamline processes, ensuring that all activities are executed efficiently and on time.

Managing the scope of such a massive event involves defining and controlling what is included and excluded. The scope management ensures that all planned activities are completed within the set boundaries, avoiding scope creep. This is crucial for maintaining focus and achieving the event's objectives.

MahaKumbh 2025 is structured as a multi-layered program with multiple workstreams, each functioning as a separate project:

- **Infrastructure & City Planning:** Roads, sanitation, power grids, water supply, etc.

- **Pilgrim Management:** Accommodation, crowd movement, public safety, etc.

- **Security & Surveillance:** Law enforcement, digital monitoring, emergency response, etc.

- **Religious & Cultural Events:** Processions, rituals, discourses by saints, etc.

- **Commercial & Economic Management:** Vendor allocation, economic impact assessment, etc.

- **Technology & Digital Governance:** AI-based analytics, online registration, live tracking, etc.

Budgeting & Cost Management

With a budget allocation, the event showcases exemplary cost management and budgeting practices. The funds are distributed across various needs, such as infrastructure, security, healthcare, and digital services.

The effective allocation of resources demonstrates intelligent budgeting and financial oversight, ensuring the event runs smoothly and meets all requirements.

Managing an event of this scale requires meticulous financial planning and resource allocation.

The event budget for MahaKumbh 2025 was estimated at Rs.7500 crore by the state and central government, covering:

- Infrastructure development (40%)

- Security & surveillance (15%)

- Sanitation & waste management (10%)

- Accommodation & transport (20%)

- Technology integration (5%)

- Contingency & risk mitigation (10%)

Revenue Generation

The Maha Kumbh Mela 2025 in Prayagraj has emerged as a monumental event, both spiritually and economically. According to Praveen Khandelwal, Secretary General of the Confederation of All India Traders (CAIT), the festival has generated over Rs.3 lakh crore in business transactions as projected of Rs.2 lakh crore. This substantial economic activity is attributed to the participation of 65 crore (650 million) devotees, with an average expenditure of Rs.5,000 per individual.

The influx of pilgrims has significantly boosted various sectors, including hospitality, food and beverages, religious artifacts, healthcare, and other essential services. Notably, the sale of religious offerings and items, such as incense sticks, lamps, and idols, has been a key contributor to the overall trade volume. This financial surge has not only invigorated local businesses but has also made a considerable impact on the state's economic landscape.

This financial influx has significantly bolstered various sectors, contributing to the state's economic growth:

Accommodation and Tourism: The influx of pilgrims led to a surge in demand for lodging, from luxury hotels to temporary tents, generating around Rs.40,000 crore

Food and Beverages: Consumption of meals, snacks, and beverages by attendees contributed approximately Rs.20,000 crore

Religious Items and Offerings: Sales of items such as idols, incense sticks, and ritual materials amounted to about Rs.20,000 crore

Transportation and Logistics: Enhanced travel services, including local transit and interstate transport, accounted for nearly Rs.10,000 crore

Tourism Services: Guided tours and travel packages added an estimated Rs.10,000 crore to the economy

Handicrafts and Souvenirs: Artisans and vendors saw sales of crafts and memorabilia totalling around Rs.5,000 crore

Healthcare Services: Medical camps and wellness services provided during the event generated close to Rs.3,000 crore

IT and Digital Services: Digital payments, e-ticketing, and Wi-Fi provisions contributed approximately Rs.1,000 crore

Entertainment and Media: Advertising, promotions, and media coverage resulted in revenues of about Rs.10,000 crore

These figures highlight the extensive economic impact of the Maha Kumbh Mela 2025, showcasing its role as a catalyst for growth across multiple industries.

Data Collection, Probability Model, & Risk Mitigation

Historical data from previous Kumbh Melas has been analyzed for effective decision-making, though certain parameters may not hold relevance due to changing demographics, climate conditions, and technological advancements.

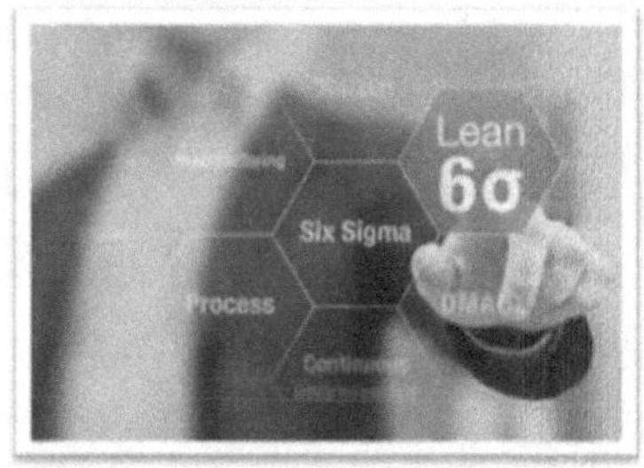

To ensure precise execution, a Probability Model with a 95% Confidence Interval might have been applied. However, considering the casualty rate due to unforeseen stampede incidents at the MahaKumbh area—where the officially recorded loss of life stood at 30 compared to the footfall above 650Million (>65 crores)—the Sigma value for life safety exceeded 6 Sigma, as defined by Motorola and GE in the 1980s and 1990s.

A process achieves Six Sigma when defects are limited to 3.4 per million opportunities. In this context demonstrating safety performance surpasses Six Sigma standards.

Key considerations in the probability model included:

- Pilgrim arrival patterns derived from historical data of previous events

- Impact of weather conditions on crowd behavior and movement dynamics

- Identification of transportation bottlenecks and optimization of traffic flow

- Accurate estimation of food and water demand to meet logistical challenges

- Emergency evacuation planning to enhance responsiveness and risk mitigation

This data-driven approach ensured efficient event planning, crowd management, and safety protocols, minimizing risks while accommodating the unprecedented scale of attendees.

Risk Management & Quality Control

Risk management involves identifying, analyzing, and mitigating potential risks. The MahaKumbh's risk management plan includes safety protocols, emergency response plans, and contingency measures. This proactive approach ensures that any

unforeseen issues are promptly addressed, minimizing disruptions.

Quality management ensures that all aspects of the event meet the highest standards. From the construction of temporary structures to the delivery of digital services, every component undergoes rigorous quality checks. This commitment to quality ensures a superior experience for all attendees.

Given the complexity of MahaKumbh, several risks are assessed and mitigated:

- **Crowd Management:** AI-based monitoring, real-time alerts

- **Health & Safety:** Medical camps, ambulance corridors

- **Environmental Hazards:** Ganga pollution control, sanitation drive

- **Security Threats:** Multi-layered surveillance, cyber-security for digital transactions, etc.

- **Weather Disruptions:** Alternate site plans, infrastructure resilience, etc.

Procurement Management

Procurement management ensures that all necessary goods and services are acquired from reliable vendors. This involves negotiating contracts, managing supplier relationships, and ensuring timely delivery. Effective procurement management is essential for the smooth functioning of the event.

First Time Right – Lean Six Sigma Implementation

The principle of First Time Right ensures that tasks are completed correctly the first time, reducing the need for rework and improving efficiency. This principle is applied across various aspects of the event, from infrastructure development to digital services.

Applying Lean Six Sigma principles ensures efficiency and zero-defect execution:

- **5S Implementation (Sort, Set in Order, Shine, Standardize, Sustain)** in crowd control, waste management, and facility maintenance

- **TIMWOODS (Transportation, Inventory, Motion, Wait-Time, Over-Processing, Over-Production, Defect, Skill-set)** to eliminate waste in processes

- **Value Stream Mapping (VSM)** to identify the Non-Value adds and streamline the process

- **First Time Right (FTR) Approach** for critical operations like water supply, sanitation, and transportation

- **Kaizen Approach** for continuous improvement in logistics, security, and waste management

Time & Resource Optimization

Time management is critical to the success of the MahaKumbh. Detailed schedules and timelines are created for every activity, ensuring that everything is completed on time.

The use of project management tools and techniques helps keep track of progress and deadlines.

With an unprecedented footfall, time management is critical:

- Scheduling pilgrim movements to avoid overcrowding

- Real-time traffic diversions for seamless transport

- Automated ticketing and QR-based identification to reduce waiting time

- Digitized communication strategies for quick information dissemination

- Visual Management using sign boards, banners, etc for quick understanding, and proactive problem-solving by making processes transparent and readily visible to everyone

Vendor Management

Vendor Management involves overseeing and coordinating relationships with suppliers to ensure that services and products are delivered efficiently and effectively. In the context of MahaKumbh 2025, vendor management is crucial due to the large-scale procurement and logistics required. This includes negotiating contracts, ensuring compliance with terms, monitoring performance, and maintaining open communication channels. With thousands of vendors providing food, lodging, transportation, utilities, and religious items, ensuring quality, timely delivery, and regulatory compliance was a key challenge.

- **Vendor Registration & Categorization**:
    - Digital vendor registration ensured transparency
    - Categorization was done for food stalls, tent accommodations, sanitation providers, transport services, and security contractors

- o RFID-enabled tracking for vendor locations and movement

- **Performance Monitoring & Compliance:**
  - o Each vendor had to meet predefined service-level agreements (SLAs)
  - o Regular quality audits and crowd feedback surveys ensured adherence
  - o AI-powered surveillance monitored hygiene and food safety standards

- **Example: Food Vendors**
  - o Over 10,000 food stalls operated, serving 650+ million meals
  - o Real-time supply chain tracking ensured zero food shortages
  - o GPS-enabled logistics-optimized delivery of raw materials

Stakeholder Management in MahaKumbh 2025

Stakeholder Management is the systematic identification, analysis, and engagement of stakeholders to ensure their needs and expectations are met. At MahaKumbh 2025, stakeholders range from government officials and local communities to vendors and pilgrims.

Identifying Key Stakeholders

The event had diverse stakeholders, including:

1. Government Bodies (Central & State Governments, Local Authorities, Police, Disaster Response Teams, etc.)

2. Religious Groups & Akharas (13 Akharas, Saints, Naga Sadhus, etc.)

3. Pilgrims & Tourists (Indian & International Visitors)

4. Vendors & Businesses (Food, Lodging, Transport, Utilities, Healthcare, etc.)

5. Media & Digital Platforms (News Agencies, Influencers, Social Media Teams)

Communication Matrix and Models

A Communication Matrix outlines how information is shared among team members and stakeholders. It ensures that the right people receive the right information at the right time.

1. RACI Model (Responsible, Accountable, Consulted, Informed)
2. ARMI Model (Approver, Resource, Member, and Interested Party)
3. RASIC Model (Responsible, Approve, Support, Inform, Consult)

Establishing Clear Communication Channels

A foundational element of the communication matrix was the delineation of clear communication channels. By defining specific pathways for information flow, teams could efficiently share

updates, directives, and feedback. This clarity minimized misunderstandings and ensured that all stakeholders were consistently informed. For instance, regular interdepartmental meetings and briefings were scheduled to synchronize efforts across different sectors involved in the Mela.

Role Definition and Accountability

The communication model also emphasized the importance of clearly defined roles and responsibilities. Each team, whether it was responsible for infrastructure, security, health services, or crowd management, had specific duties outlined.

This precision not only streamlined operations but also established accountability, ensuring that tasks were executed effectively and any issues were promptly addressed.

Integration of Advanced Communication Tools

To support the extensive communication requirements, the Department of Telecommunications (DoT), in collaboration with various service providers, augmented the telecom infrastructure across Prayagraj. This enhancement included the installation of over 900 new Base Transceiver Stations (BTS), the upgrading of more than 1,550 existing BTS units, and deploying 78 transportable towers and 150 small cell solutions. These efforts ensured robust and uninterrupted connectivity, which was crucial for real-time coordination among teams and for disseminating information to the public.

Implementation of Emergency Communication Protocols

Recognizing the potential for emergencies in such a large gathering, the communication matrix incorporated protocols for crises. A Cell Broadcast Alert facility was established to send emergency alerts,

disaster warnings, and public awareness messages. Additionally, three disaster management centers were set up within the Mela area to support emergency communications and ensure prompt responses during crises.

Citizen-Centric Communication Services

To further enhance public safety and convenience, 53 help desks were established throughout the Mela area. These centers provided services such as reporting fraudulent communications and assistance with lost or stolen mobile devices. This initiative not only aided in maintaining security but also fostered a sense of trust and reliability among attendees.

The structured communication matrix/model was instrumental in orchestrating the collaborative efforts of various teams during the Maha Kumbh Mela 2025. By establishing clear communication channels, defining roles, integrating advanced tools, and implementing emergency protocols, the event was managed efficiently, ensuring a safe and enriching experience for all participants.

Market Basket Analysis and Its Application to MahaKumbh 2025

Market Basket Analysis (MBA) is a data-driven technique used in analytics to identify purchasing patterns by examining the relationships between items frequently bought together. It helps in understanding consumer behavior, optimizing product placement, and enhancing business strategies. Traditionally used in retail and e-commerce, MBA can also be applied to large-scale events like MahaKumbh 2025, where millions of people gather, leading to complex demand patterns across various sectors.

Market Basket Analysis in MahaKumbh 2025

Given the sheer scale of the MahaKumbh, with an expected footfall of over 650 million people, MBA plays a crucial role in predicting, organizing, and optimizing resource allocation. The event is a massive ecosystem of religious, commercial, and logistical activities, making it an ideal case study for analyzing visitor behavior and economic impact.

Key Applications of MBA in MahaKumbh

1. **Pilgrim Spending Patterns**

   o Visitors often purchase prasad, rudraksha beads, holy books, idols, incense sticks, and lamps together

   o Religious tourism packages typically bundle accommodations, food, local transport, and guided tours

   o Devotees attending Amrit Snan (Shahi Snan) may also seek purification kits, saffron robes, and spiritual souvenirs

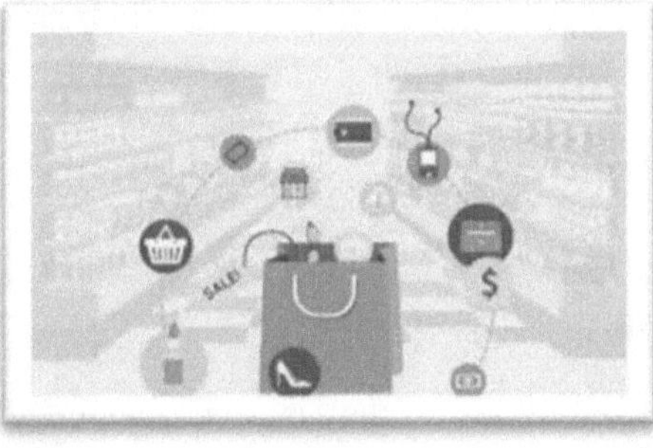

2. **Food and Beverage Consumption**

   o Market Basket Analysis can help identify popular food combinations, such as pilgrims purchasing tea and snacks together or opting for thali meals

o   Langars (community kitchens) and street food stalls can optimize their supply chains by analyzing which food items are frequently consumed together

3.   Transportation & Mobility

o   Pilgrims travelling in groups tend to book buses, e-rickshaws, and boats together to move across key sites such as Sangam Nose, Arail Ghat, Kila Ghat, Akshay Vat, and Hanuman Mandir

o   Data can help authorities improve traffic flow and shuttle services, reducing congestion and ensuring a smoother experience

4.   Accommodation & Religious Events

o   Temporary tent cities offer various amenities, and MBA can predict what services are frequently booked together (e.g., premium accommodations with access to VIP darshan and meditation spaces)

o   Foreign pilgrims may prefer packages that include multilingual guides, heritage walks, boats, and boat house

5.   Medical & Emergency Services

o   Identifying common medical needs (e.g., dehydration medicines, first aid, and Ayurveda-based remedies) can help set up well-equipped health kiosks at strategic locations

  o High-traffic zones like bathing ghats can be analyzed to deploy ambulances and emergency teams effectively

Architectural Alignment and Temporary City Design

The MahaKumbh Mela Ground is transformed into a meticulously planned temporary city, integrating market basket insights into its architectural layout to ensure seamless pilgrim experiences.

1. Zoning Based on Visitor Behavior

- **Sacred Zone:** Includes the Triveni Sangam, Arail Ghat, Akshay Vat, and major temples, ensuring easy access to religious spots

- **Commercial Zone:** Houses shops for puja items, food stalls, souvenir markets, and handicraft vendors, positioned based on expected foot traffic

- **Hospitality Zone:** Includes tent cities, Dharamshala, hotels, and community lodges, arranged to accommodate different budget ranges

- **Transportation Hubs:** Strategically placed shuttle stops, bus terminals, and boat docks to facilitate movement across the city

2. Data-Driven City Planning

- Using past footfall analytics, pathways and roads have been widened to prevent congestion and to manage traffic on the highways connecting to Prayagraj

- Bathing ghats have been redesigned with dedicated entry and exit points to reduce overcrowding

- Smart surveillance systems track crowd movement and redirect flow during peak hours

MahaKumbh 2025: A Case Study in Agile Event Management and Urban Planning

MahaKumbh 2025 stands as an extraordinary real-world application of Market Basket Analysis, extending beyond its traditional role in retail to influence event administration, economic structuring, and urban planning.

By leveraging pilgrim behavior data and spending trends, authorities and businesses optimized resource distribution, trade opportunities, and operational logistics, ensuring a seamless experience for millions of devotees.

This data-driven approach, combined with spiritual traditions, highlights Bharat's ability to blend technology with cultural heritage, positioning MahaKumbh not just as a sacred congregation but as a global benchmark for large-scale event management and infrastructure development.

Agile Framework in MahaKumbh 2025: Dynamic Event Administration

Given the dynamic and unpredictable nature of an event that attracts over 650 million visitors, the Agile framework was crucial in ensuring real-time decision-making, risk mitigation, and adaptive planning.

The event administration followed Agile principles by breaking down massive logistical operations into smaller, more manageable units and responding proactively to on-ground challenges.

Key Agile Applications in MahaKumbh 2025

1. **Sprint-Based Crowd Management**

   o Authorities worked in short sprints to monitor crowd density, adjusting routes, diversions, and barricades in real time

   o Live data dashboards enabled administrators to deploy additional personnel and redirect pilgrims to less crowded zones efficiently

2. **Traffic Flow Optimization**

   o IoT-enabled traffic monitoring systems provided real-time congestion alerts, allowing traffic controllers to adjust vehicle routes dynamically

o Temporary road expansions, pedestrian-only zones, and shuttle services were modified on an iterative basis to decongest high-traffic areas

3. **Emergency Response & Risk Mitigation**

o Incident response teams followed a SCRUM approach, working in cross-functional squads to address medical emergencies, lost pilgrims, and overcrowding

o The Command-and-Control Center used real-time drone surveillance and predictive analytics to pre-emptively identify potential risks and dispatch resources accordingly

4. **Adaptive Resource Allocation**

o Food distribution centers, water supply points, and sanitation facilities were continuously reassessed using demand forecasting models, ensuring a balanced supply throughout the mela grounds

o Pilgrim behavior analytics helped identify peak hours for specific zones, enabling on-the-go adjustments in resource availability

5. **Iterative Improvement Through Continuous Feedback**

o Pilgrim feedback mechanisms, including mobile apps and kiosks, provided real-time insights into problem areas

- o Daily retrospectives among administrative teams ensured that lessons learned from one day's operations were immediately implemented the next day

A Blueprint for Future Mega Events

MahaKumbh 2025 is a testament to Bharat's operational excellence, serving as an ideal case study for corporate leaders, policymakers, and urban planners worldwide. It transcends a spiritual gathering, evolving into a fusion of faith, engineering, Agile governance, and Digital Transformation.

While devotees experienced a divine and spiritually uplifting journey, professionals in management, logistics, and urban development recognized MahaKumbh as a masterpiece of strategic execution, cost optimization, and real-time decision-making. The Agile-led administration demonstrated how faith, governance, and advanced technology can work in perfect synergy to orchestrate an event of unprecedented scale and complexity.

MahaKumbh 2025 is not merely a religious event—it is a living model of Agile Event Management, a global reference for handling massive gatherings through data-driven, iterative, and responsive planning strategies.

Quick Action Teams (QAT): Real-Time Issue Resolution

Given the unpredictable nature of MahaKumbh, Quick Action Teams (QATs) played a critical role in handling emergencies like stampedes, overcrowding, medical aid, and logistical failures.

Key Features of QATs in MahaKumbh 2025

- 24/7 Monitoring: Teams were stationed at critical points across the mela
- AI & Drone Support: Drones provided real-time crowd density analysis
- Medical Response Teams: Equipped with ambulances, paramedics, and mobile clinics
- Traffic Redirection Teams: RFID-based vehicle tracking helped reroute traffic in congestion-prone areas

Example: QAT in Action During Overcrowding at Sangam

Situation: A sudden influx of 5 million devotees at Sangam Nose created congestion risks.

QAT Response:

- Drone surveillance detected density spikes, triggering immediate alerts

- Alternative entry/exit routes were opened within 10 minutes

- Announcements & App Alerts directed pilgrims to less crowded areas

- Local police deployed barricades, preventing a potential stampede

A Masterclass in Large-Scale Management

The flawless execution of MahaKumbh 2025 was a result of precise Vendor Management, structured Stakeholder Engagement, Strategic Communication Models, and the proactive deployment of Quick Action Teams (QATs).

- The RACI, ARMI, and RASIC models helped define responsibilities, ensuring every team worked in coordination

- Real-time decision-making, supported by AI, drones, and IoT, allowed quick responses to congestion and emergencies

- Stakeholder alignment between the government, religious authorities, and local businesses ensured a harmonious and well-coordinated event

MahaKumbh 2025 is a living case study that showcases how spiritual gatherings can be managed with cutting-edge technology, agile decision-making, and structured governance frameworks. It sets a global benchmark for managing mass events with efficiency, safety, and cultural reverence.

Digital Marketing Strategies for MahaKumbh 2025

The MahaKumbh 2025 in Prayagraj exemplifies Bharat's remarkable fusion of age-old traditions with contemporary technology. This blend is notably showcased through the digital marketing efforts that highlight the event's wide range of activities, such as drone shows, light displays, and cultural performances.

1. Social Media Engagement

Recognizing the pervasive influence of social media, organizers launched comprehensive campaigns across platforms such as Facebook, Instagram, and Twitter. These campaigns featured captivating visuals and teasers of upcoming events, effectively engaging a global audience and fostering a sense of anticipation.

2. Influencer Collaborations

To amplify reach, partnerships were established with prominent influencers and spiritual leaders. These collaborations provided authentic insights and personal experiences related to the MahaKumbh, resonating deeply with both existing devotees and potential visitors

3. Virtual Reality (VR) Experiences

Embracing cutting-edge technology, 360-degree virtual reality stalls were set up at prime locations within the Kumbh Mela area. These installations allowed visitors to immerse themselves in key events such as the Peshwai (grand procession) and Ganga Aarti, offering a unique and accessible perspective of the festival's highlights

4. Dedicated Mobile Applications

A specialized mobile app was developed to serve as a centralized hub for information and engagement. The app provided real-time updates, event schedules, and interactive maps, enhancing the overall experience for attendees and virtual participants alike.

5. Email Marketing Campaigns

Targeted email campaigns were employed to disseminate personalized content, including event highlights, exclusive interviews, and behind-the-scenes glimpses. This approach fostered a deeper connection with the audience, encouraging active participation and sustained interest

Promoting Key Events Through Digital Platforms

Drone and Light Shows

A standout feature of MahaKumbh 2025 was the drone light show, where a fleet of 2,000 illuminated drones narrated vedic tales such as the Samudra Manthan and the emergence of the Amrit Kalash. This mesmerizing display was extensively promoted through social media teasers, live-streaming events, and collaborative posts with tech influencers, generating widespread excitement and engagement

Cultural and Musical Performances

The festival's rich tapestry of cultural and musical events was highlighted through a series of digital initiatives:

- **Artist Spotlights**: Profiles and interviews of participating artists were shared on social media, offering insights into their craft and enhancing audience connection

- **Interactive Sessions**: Virtual Q&A sessions and workshops were organized, enabling enthusiasts to engage directly with performers and gain a deeper appreciation of the cultural heritage showcased at the MahaKumbh

Influencer and Independent Content Creator Collaborations

Recognizing the influential power of digital personalities, the MahaKumbh 2025 organizers have partnered with a range of influencers and content creators to amplify the festival's presence across various platforms:

- **Spiritual Influencers**: Individuals such as Sadhviji Hindi, a former Hollywood writer turned spiritual guru, have been sharing immersive content that captures the essence of the MahaKumbh, blending ancient wisdom with contemporary digital storytelling

- **Travel and Lifestyle Bloggers**: Creators and several other bloggers have been documenting their experiences at the festival, providing followers with virtual tours and personal insights, thereby enticing a broader audience to engage with the event

- **International Content Creators**: Teams of YouTubers from countries such as Japan, South America, and South Africa have been broadcasting the grandeur of the MahaKumbh to a global audience, showcasing the festival's universal appeal

Digital Marketing Initiatives

To further enhance the festival's digital footprint, several strategic initiatives have been implemented:

- **Interactive Social Media Campaigns**: The Ministry of Tourism has launched engaging campaigns featuring interactive polls and immersive content, targeting a global audience to raise awareness about the MahaKumbh 2025

- **Live Streaming and Virtual Participation**: Major events, including the drone and light shows, have been live-streamed across platforms like YouTube and Facebook Live, allowing virtual attendees worldwide to partake in the festivities

- **User-Generated Content Encouragement**: Attendees and virtual participants are encouraged to share their experiences using event-specific hashtags (like #MahaKumbh2025 & #mahakumbh), creating a vibrant online community and extending the festival's reach

Through these multifaceted digital marketing strategies, including the significant contributions of social media influencers and independent content creators, MahaKumbh 2025 has not only honored its profound spiritual roots but also embraced contemporary technological advancements.

This harmonious blend has ensured that the festival resonates with a diverse, global audience, setting a precedent for future cultural events.

Maha Kumbh 2025:

A Global Confluence of Spirituality and Unity

The Maha Kumbh Mela 2025, held in Prayagraj, Bharat (India), transcended its spiritual essence to become a universal symbol of unity and cultural confluence. Attracting millions of devotees, seekers, and global leaders from diverse faiths and nationalities, the event showcased the ancient Bhartiya (Indian) principle of **"Vasudhaiva Kutumbakam"—the world is one family**.

One of the most revered gatherings in human history, the MahaKumbh embodies inclusivity. The belief that "Kumbh me sab aate hain" (Everyone comes to Kumbh) reflects its spiritual magnetism, drawing individuals from all walks of life.

As one saint profoundly stated: *"Brahma ji ne jab insaan ki rachna ki to wo Sanatani hi tha, ataha Vishwa me sabhi Sanatani hain kyonki Prithvi me aakar hi log jaati dharm me bat jaate hain" (When Lord Brahma created humans, they were all Sanatani (eternal). It is upon arriving on Earth that they divide into castes and religions)."*

An Unparalleled Global Gathering

In 2025, the Maha Kumbh welcomed over 650 million pilgrims and saw participation from global dignitaries, spiritual leaders, and celebrities worldwide. This influx reinforced the Kumbh's role as a religious congregation and a universal celebration of faith, devotion, and culture.

Global Figures and Their Spiritual Journeys at Maha Kumbh 2025

International Delegations

- **Laurene Powell Jobs (USA)**: The philanthropist and widow of Steve Jobs attended Maha Kumbh, deeply resonating with its spiritual energy and philosophy

- **Richard Gere (USA)**: The American actor and humanitarian attended the Maha Kumbh, reflecting his long-standing interest in Eastern philosophies and spirituality

- **Pieter Elbers (CEO IndiGo)** said, "I took the holy early morning dip at 5 am in the sacred confluence of rivers, the holy Sangam with about a million at the same time, surrounded by chants, prayers, devotion and the unity of humanity. Found an inexplicable moment of peace in the chaos,"

- **Daniel Radcliffe (UK):** The British actor, best known for his role as Harry Potter, made a brief visit to the Kumbh Mela, immersing himself in the spiritual ambience of the event

- **Chris Martin (UK)**: The British musician and lead vocalist of Coldplay made a brief visit to the Kumbh Mela, immersing himself in the spiritual ambience of the event

- **14th Dalai Lama:** "We human beings depend on each other and must live together on this one planet that is our only home," his message highlighted the shared foundations of religious traditions, noting that they all emphasise "cultivating love and compassion in our daily lives."

- **Yogmata Keiko Aikawa (Japan):** The Japanese spiritual master, Yogmata Keiko Aikawa, attended the Maha Kumbh, sharing her teachings and participating in the holy dip at the Triveni Sangam

- **68 Hindu Devotees from Pakistan's Sindh Province**: A group of 68 Hindu devotees from Pakistan's Sindh province arrived at the Maha Kumbh, symbolizing cross-border spiritual ties and the universal nature of the festival

- **Diplomats from 73 Countries**: A diverse group of diplomats from countries including Russia, Ukraine, Japan, USA, Germany, and Canada attended the Maha Kumbh Mela, witnessing the grandeur of the event and participating in its spiritual activities

- **Over 660 Buddhist Devotees from Eight Nations**: Buddhist practitioners from Thailand, Sri Lanka, Myanmar, Bhutan, Japan, Vietnam, Cambodia, and Mongolia participated in the Maha Kumbh, transforming the festival into a global spiritual confluence and highlighting Bharat's role as a unifying force in spirituality

Business Sector

- **Gautam Adani (Bharat/India)**: The industrialist visited the Triveni Sangam to offer prayers, and visited Bade Hanuman ji with his family

- **Mukesh Ambani (Bharat/India)**: The Chairman and Managing Director of Reliance Industries Limited, Mukesh

Ambani, visited the Triveni Sangam to offer prayers, underscoring the blend of spirituality and leadership

- **Ronojoy Dutta (Bharat/India)**: The Former CEO of IndiGo Airlines, Ronojoy Dutta, attended the Kumbh Mela, reflecting the aviation industry's recognition of the event's significance

- **Sudha Murthy (Bharat/India)**: The renowned author and philanthropist, Sudha Murthy, participated in the Kumbh Mela, emphasizing her commitment to cultural and spiritual traditions

A Confluence of Faiths and Cultures

The 2025 Maha Kumbh has not only been a focal point for Hindu devotees but has also welcomed participants from various religious backgrounds:

- **Interfaith Participation:** Individuals from Christian, Muslim, Buddhist, and other faiths attended, drawn by the event's spiritual energy and cultural richness

- **Cultural Exchange:** The presence of international visitors facilitated a vibrant exchange of traditions, fostering global unity and understanding

- **Sikh Gurus** – Prominent Sikh leaders from Amritsar and abroad highlighted the shared essence of devotion in all faiths

The Essence of Vasudhaiva Kutumbakam

The Maha Kumbh Mela 2025 stands as a living example of Bharat's (India) ancient yet ever-relevant ethos of inclusivity, peace, spirituality, tradition, modern management, and practices of cultural integration. It is not just a religious event but a testament to human unity, reinforcing that beyond borders, faiths, and nationalities, we are all connected.

As one saint beautifully summarized:
"The Ganges does not ask who you are before granting you purification. It simply embraces all who come to it. Such is the greatness of Sanatan Dharma, and such is the spirit of Maha Kumbh."

In a world increasingly divided by differences, Maha Kumbh 2025 has reaffirmed the fundamental truth that humanity is one.

It is a festival where faith unites, culture blends, and the world becomes a family—**Vasudhaiva Kutumbakam** in its truest sense.

Amrit Vachan – Teachings of Spiritual Awakening & Devotion

At the Mahakumbh in Prayagraj, several esteemed spiritual leaders delivered profound discourses, offering guidance and inspiration to millions of devotees. Here are some notable highlights:

Swami Avdheshanand Giri – Embracing Inner Peace

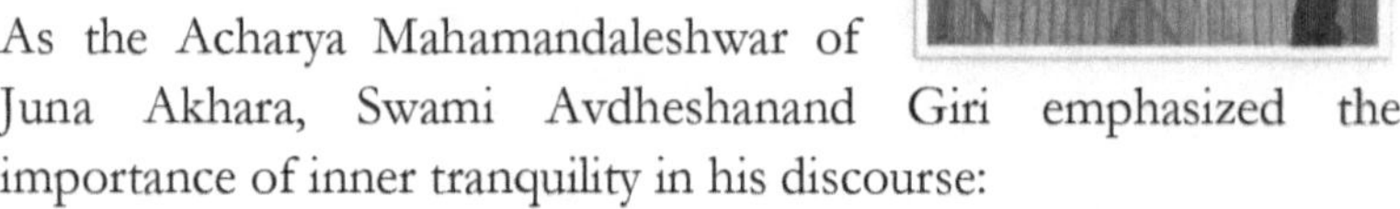

As the Acharya Mahamandaleshwar of Juna Akhara, Swami Avdheshanand Giri emphasized the importance of inner tranquility in his discourse:

"सच्ची शांति बाहरी परिस्थितियों में नहीं, बल्कि हमारे स्वयं के हृदय की गहराइयों में पाई जाती है। ईश्वर का ध्यान और सांसारिक इच्छाओं से विरक्ति ही हमें स्थायी शांति की ओर ले जाती है।"

"True peace is not found in external circumstances but within the depths of our own hearts. By meditating on the divine and detaching from material desires, we can attain lasting serenity."

Swami Nischalananda Saraswati – The Path of Righteousness

The 145th Shankaracharya of Puri Govardhan Peeth, Swami Nischalananda Saraswati, spoke about adhering to dharma:

"इन नैतिक अनिश्चितता के समय में, धर्म के प्रति अडिग रहना हमारे मार्ग को प्रकाशमान करता है और हमें आध्यात्मिक संतुष्टि व सामाजिक समरसता की ओर ले जाता है।"

"In these times of moral uncertainty, steadfastness in one's dharma (righteous duty) serves as the guiding light, leading us toward spiritual fulfillment and societal harmony."

Swami Ramabhadracharya – Devotion Through Selfless Service

Founder of Tulsi Peeth and revered Jagadguru Ramanandacharya, Swami Ramabhadracharya, highlighted the essence of selfless service:

"निस्वार्थ सेवा आत्मा को शुद्ध करती है और हमें परमात्मा के समीप ले जाती है। हमारे सभी कर्म ईश्वर के चरणों में समर्पित होने चाहिए।"

"Serving others without expectation purifies the soul and brings us closer to the Divine. Let our actions be offerings at the feet of the Almighty."

Swami Ramdev – Health as a Spiritual Practice

Renowned yoga guru Swami Ramdev linked physical well-being to spiritual growth:

"एक स्वस्थ शरीर एक स्पष्ट मन को जन्म देता है, जो आध्यात्मिक साधना के लिए अनिवार्य है। योग और प्राणायाम के माध्यम से हम अपने शरीर और आत्मा को संतुलित कर सकते हैं, जो आत्मज्ञान का मार्ग प्रशस्त करता है।"

"A healthy body fosters a clear mind, which is essential for spiritual practices. Through yoga and pranayama, we align our physical and spiritual selves, paving the way to enlightenment."

Gurudev Sri Sri Ravi Shankar – Unity in Diversity

Founder of the Art of Living Foundation, Gurudev Sri Sri Ravi Shankar, spoke on universal harmony:

"इस विशाल सृष्टि में प्रत्येक व्यक्ति एक अनोखा धागा है। प्रेमपूर्वक विविधताओं को अपनाने से समाज में समरसता और समृद्धि आती है।"

"In the vast tapestry of creation, every individual is a unique thread. Embracing our differences with love leads to a harmonious and enriched society."

Saints' Teachings

Devraha Baba (Stated early 90's)

"कुंभ में सभी आते हैं – देव, दानव, गंधर्व, भूत, भगवान, और मनुष्य।"

"Kumbh welcomes all—Devas, Asuras, Gandharvas, spirits, divine beings, and humans."

Premanand Ji Maharaj

"कुंभ में जाओ तो जितना हो सके मौन को धारण करो, साधु-संतों के अमृत ज्ञान से अपने मन-मस्तिष्क को धन्य करो।"

"While attending Kumbh, maintain as much silence as possible, and absorb the divine wisdom of saints and sages."

Gautam Buddha (Arya Maun – The Power of Noble Silence)

"मौन एक महान साधना है, जो आत्मज्ञान की ओर ले जाती है।"

"Silence is a profound practice that leads to self-realization."

Swami Kailashanand Giri Maharaj

"अमृत स्नान आत्मशुद्धि और आध्यात्मिक जागरण का एक महत्वपूर्ण अवसर है।"

"The holy dip at Kumbh is an opportunity for self-purification and spiritual awakening."

💧 On Renunciation & Detachment (Vairagya) –

"जो सबको अपना मानता है, वह कभी अकेला नहीं होता।"

"One who sees everyone as their own is never alone."

"संसार एक भ्रम है, और इससे मुक्ति ही परम सुख है।"

"The world is an illusion, and liberation from it is the ultimate bliss."

"वैराग्य तब आता है जब मन विषयों से ऊपर उठ जाए।"

"Detachment arises when the mind rises above material desires."

"जितना देह का मोह कम होगा, उतनी ही आत्मा की चेतना जागृत होगी।"

"The less attachment to the body, the more awakened the soul becomes."

The Significance of the Holy Dip at Sangam

"गंगा सिर्फ एक नदी नहीं, यह आत्मा की शुद्धि का एक माध्यम है।"

"The Ganga is not just a river; it is a medium for soul purification."

"त्रिवेणी संगम का स्नान शरीर को नहीं, आत्मा को पवित्र करता है।"

"The sacred dip at Triveni Sangam purifies not the body, but the soul."

"जल में प्रवेश सिर्फ शारीरिक नहीं, यह मन और विचारों की शुद्धिकरण यात्रा है।"

"Entering the holy waters is not just a physical act but a journey of mental and spiritual purification."

On Mind, Yoga & Self-Realization

"मन को शांत करने का एक ही मंत्र है—योग और ध्यान।"

"The only mantra to calm the mind is Yoga and Meditation."

"जो अपनी आत्मा के स्वरूप को पहचान लेता है, उसका सारा दुख मिट जाता है।"

"One who realizes the true nature of the soul is free from all suffering."

"मोक्ष पाने की चिंता मत करो, अपने कर्म सुधारो।"

"Do not worry about liberation; focus on improving your actions."

On Dharma & Righteous Living

"धर्म सिर्फ ग्रंथों में नहीं, जीवन के हर कर्म में होना चाहिए।"

"Dharma is not just in scriptures; it should reflect in every action of life."

"जो सत्य को धारण करता है, वही असली तपस्वी है।"

"One who upholds truth is the real ascetic."

"अहिंसा के बिना कोई भी धर्म संपूर्ण नहीं है।"

"No religion is complete without non-violence."

Bharat – The Land of Spirituality & Wisdom

"भारत सिर्फ एक देश नहीं, यह धर्म की भूमि और तपस्या का केंद्र है।"

"Bharat is not just a country; it is the land of dharma and spiritual penance."

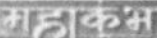

The divine discourses of saints and sages at MahaKumbh illuminated the path of spirituality, devotion, righteousness, selfless service, and universal harmony.

These timeless teachings inspire seekers on their journey toward self-realization, inner peace, and ultimate liberation.

"वसुधैव कुटुंबकम्" – "The whole world is one family."

Photo Gallery

#MAHAKUMBH2025

Appendix: Reference & Source

Primary Scriptural Sources

1. Bhagavata Purana (Srimad Bhagavatam) – Describes the Samudra Manthan and the battle for Amrit
2. Matsya Purana – Details sacred rivers and Kumbh locations
3. Mahabharata (Vana Parva, Chapter 85-86) – Mentions the celestial significance of Kumbh
4. Brahmanda Purana – Discusses the astrological importance of the Kumbh cycle

Historical Mentions

1. Al-Biruni (Persian Historian, 1030 CE) - Documented the Kumbh at Prayagraj
2. Hiuen Tsang (Chinese Traveler, 7th Century CE) – Noted Emperor Harsha's grand Kumbh Mela
3. British Colonial Records (19th-20th Century CE) – Official documentation of Kumbh Melas

Books for Reference

1. "Kumbh Mela: Mapping the Ephemeral Mega City" – Tarun Khanna & Rahul Mehrotra
   o Analysis of Kumbh Mela's organization and the role of Akharas
2. "The Kumbh Mela: Pilgrimage and the Hindu Tradition" – D.P. Dubey
   o History, rituals, and significance of Akharas at Kumbh Mela
3. "Sadhus: Holy Men of India" – Dolf Hartsuiker
   o Insights into Naga Sadhus and various ascetic sects

4. "Hindu Monastic Life: The Monks and Monasteries of Bhubaneswar" – Edward Balfour
   o Detailed study of Akharas and monastic traditions
5. "Shaiva Siddhanta: An Indian School of Mystical Thought" – N. Sundararajan
   o Traditions followed by Shaiva Akharas

Websites for Reference

1. Encyclopaedia Britannica – Covers Hindu sects, traditions, and Kumbh Mela
2. Kumbh Mela Official Website – Government-verified details of Kumbh Mela
3. Akhil Bharatiya Akhara Parishad – Information on Akharas and their role in Kumbh Mela
4. Hinduism Today – Covers Hindu traditions, including Akharas
5. Times of India – Regular reports on Kumbh Mela and related events
6. The Print India – Analytical pieces on Kumbh Mela governance

Online Articles & Reports

1. Jagran – The Beginning of Virtue Acquisition: Nashik MahaKumbh
2. Times of India – The Most Beautiful Sadhvi Takes Internet by Storm
3. Times Now Hindi – MahaKumbh Mela 2025: Anchor Harsha Richhariya Becomes Sadhvi
4. Economic Times – Viral Stories from Maha Kumbh
5. Vedic Meet – Samudra Manthan: 14 Ratnas List
6. Mokshaverse – Neelakantha Shiva
7. Mokshaverse – Samudra Manthan

8. <u>Yogapedia</u> – Understanding "Marga" in Hinduism
9. <u>News18 Hindi</u> – Akshay Vat, Prayagraj: Mythological Significance
10. <u>Press Information Bureau (PIB)</u>
11. <u>The Times UK</u> – Maha Kumbh: The World's Largest Gathering
12. <u>Reuters</u> – India's Maha Kumbh Mela 2025
13. <u>The Hans India</u> – The Spiritual Essence of Maghi Purnima
14. <u>Reuters – Holy Dip</u> – Over 500 Million Take a Holy Dip at Maha Kumbh
15. webosmotic.com - Multilingual Chatbots and Mobile Applications
16. pib.gov.in (https://pib.gov.in/PressReleasePage.aspx?PRID=2089618)
17. https://unsdg.un.org/download/171/443
18. livemint.com, zeenews.com, moneycontrol.com, hindustantimes.com – Revenue generation

Glossary

Bharat / *Hindustan* / *India* | **Prayagraj** / *Allahabad*

Maha: Biggest/Largest/Many | ***Kumbh***: Pitcher / Pot | ***Mela***: Fair/Gathering/Meet | ***Ardh***: Half |

Amrit Snan: *Royal Bath*

151

About the Author – Anilesh Mukherjee

A visionary professional in Program Management, Digital Transformation, and Corporate Strategy, Anilesh Mukherjee brings over 17 years of expertise in driving Business Transformation, Operational Excellence, Process Optimization, and AI-powered automation.

A Six Sigma Master Black Belt from the Indian Statistical Institute, he has been at the forefront of enterprise-wide transformation, leveraging AI/ML, NLP, RPA, and advanced analytics to streamline operations and unlock new growth opportunities.

Anilesh holds a Postgraduate Diploma in Management from IMT Ghaziabad and has deepened his strategic expertise through Harvard's Sustainable Strategy program. His academic foundation from Allahabad University, coupled with extensive experience in data governance, statistical modelling, and Lean Six Sigma methodologies, allows him to craft scalable, data-driven solutions that drive efficiency and agility.

As a recognized thought leader and prolific author, Anilesh has contributed to esteemed platforms such as the 'International Journal of Science and Research (IJSR)' and 'Academia' with groundbreaking insights into AI, Lean Six Sigma, and quality control innovations. His widely acclaimed works include:

- Leveraging NLP & Machine Learning for Quality Control using Lean Six Sigma (IJSR)

- The Future of Quality Control: NLP in Lean Six Sigma (Academia)
- AI's Transformation of Work, Cybersecurity & Zero Trust, Change Management, and more (LinkedIn Articles)

In 'Sacred Synergy at MahaKumbh, Uniting Spirituality, Science and Technology,' Anilesh distills his vast experience into practical frameworks and real-world case studies, equipping businesses with actionable strategies to harness AI, Agile, and digital innovation for long-term success.

With an unwavering passion for technology-led disruption, enterprise agility, and intelligent automation, he continues to shape the future of program management and digital transformation, inspiring leaders to navigate complex challenges with confidence.

जय श्री राम   ॐ नमः शिवाय   जय श्री राम

जय श्री राम   ॐ नमः शिवाय   जय श्री राम

This book culminates my experiences, research, observations, knowledge, and personal perspectives, shaped over years of exploration, learning, and introspection. Every insight, analysis, and reflection presented here is a result of my deep engagement with spirituality, science, management, and technology, merging ancient wisdom with modern advancements. While great care has been taken to ensure authenticity and accuracy, the perspectives shared are personal interpretations and should be approached as an invitation for contemplation rather than absolute conclusions.

This work's ideas, concepts, and historical references are intended to educate, inspire, and provoke thought. Any resemblance to real events or individuals, unless explicitly cited, is purely coincidental. This book is not intended as professional or legal advice.

For permissions, collaborations, or inquiries, please contact the author at anileshmukherjee1@gmail.com.

Published by Anilesh Mukherjee

First Edition, 2025

✦ Dedicated to seekers, thinkers, and visionaries shaping a future where spirituality, science, and technology converge in harmony. ✦

वसुधैव कुटुंबकम्